Religion and Diversity

European Academy of Religion (EuARe) Lectures

EuARe Executive Committee:
Karla Boersma, Francesca Cadeddu, Jocelyne Cesari,
Alessandro Ferrari, Hans-Peter Grosshans,
Pantelis Kalaitzidis, Peter Petkoff,
Herman J. Selderhuis, Kristina Stoeckl

Volume 5

Religion and Diversity

Fifth Annual Conference 2022

Edited by
Francesca Cadeddu

DE GRUYTER

ISBN 978-3-11-102611-4
e-ISBN (PDF) 978-3-11-102617-6
e-ISBN (EPUB) 978-3-11-102627-5
DOI https://doi.org/10.1515/9783111026176
ISSN 2940-455X

This work is licensed under the Creative Commons Attribution 4.0 International License.
For details go to https://creativecommons.org/licenses/by/4.0/.

Library of Congress Control Number: 2024906262

Bibliographic information published by the Deutsche Nationalbibliothek
The Deutsche Nationalbibliothek lists this publication in the Deutsche Nationalbibliografie;
detailed bibliographic data are available on the Internet at http://dnb.dnb.de.

© 2024 with the author(s), editing © Francesca Cadeddu, published by Walter de Gruyter GmbH,
Berlin/Boston. This book is published with open access at www.degruyter.com.
Printing and binding: CPI books GmbH, Leck

www.degruyter.com

Contents

Francesca Cadeddu
Introduction —— 1

Oddrun M. H. Bråten
New Social Patterns: Old Educational Structures? Comparative Perspectives on How Diversity Challenges Religious Education in Europe —— 5

David N. Hempton
From Nonsectarian to Multifaith: An Educational Experiment in Religious Diversity at Harvard ca. 1800–2020 —— 31

Halina Grzymała-Moszczyńska
The Role of Religion in Coping with Refugee Trauma: Agency and Resilience —— 51

Francesca Cadeddu
Introduction: Religion and Diversity

2022 EuARe Annual Conference

With this volume the European Academy of Religion presents the text of the Keynote Lectures that were given during its 2022 Annual Conference, held in Bologna on June 20–23, 2022. The overarching topic of the Conference for that year was "Religion and Diversity".

The EuARe – and its conferences even more so – gathers a diverse group of scholars, departments, research centres, and publishers, all with a common interest in the study and dissemination of knowledge about religions. They come from a cultural Europe, which extends far beyond the political borders of the EU and which is characterised by religious, ethnic, cultural proximities that could not be even imagined some thirty years ago.

Moreover, the issue of religious diversity has always been part of the scientific work of the hosting institution, *Fondazione per le scienze religiose* (FSCIRE), and the addition of the conjunction between the two words meant to open the topic to the widest possible public in terms of disciplines and perspectives, encouraging theological, philosophical, as well as historical, juridical, and sociological analyses.

Unfortunately, the 2022 Annual Conference took place in the geo-political context of the war between Russia and Ukraine. Scholars were questioning the role the churches played in the lack of dialogue and understanding between the conflicting parties, and they asked themselves, what role the churches played in political rhetoric that supported the conflict. The need of understanding the meaning of diversity within religions, among religions and in the cultures they inhabit seemed, at that point, of the utmost urgency.

The community of scholars gathered at the 2022 Annual Conference responded to this need with strong interest: over 800 people met in the first post-COVID19 conference of the association, describing, analysing, questioning the conference topic. The main areas of interest have ranged from interreligious dialogue and encounter to tolerance; from the impact of the pandemic on socio-juridical settings to the impact of religious practice in non-religious societies and communities; from the definition of religious groups and organisations to the relationship between faith

Francesca Cadeddu is Assistant Professor in Contemporary History at the University of Modena and Reggio Emilia and affiliated with the *Fondazione per le scienze religiose* (FSCIRE) in Bologna, Italy.

communities and political movements – all of them in different historical and geographical contexts, offering a vast panorama of disciplinary approaches and methodologies.

"Religion and Diversity" was the topic of the 2022 Annual Conference because diversity characterises internal dynamics and external relations of all religious faiths in their different dimensions: texts – in their origins, exegesis, hermeneutics, critical editions; cults – in their anthropology, aesthetics, adaptations; norms – in their sources, implementation, collection; doctrines – with their languages, narratives, transmissions; practices – in their motivation, evolution, connection or antagonism with other societal actors. Religious diversity is a complex system with multiple variants which finds its most visible reasons and outcomes in the way societies transform and represent it in their political, juridical, social systems, but also in the ways that faith communities generate dialogue or conflict within themselves and towards other communities (religious and non-religious).

The choice of lecturers at the EuARe conferences is often guided by the will to highlight European research trends and perspectives on the overarching topic, and the names chosen for the 2022 Annual Conference reflect a specific scientific interest in understanding the different ways in which European religious diversity impacted on European – and Western – history. Diversity is a condition which has produced a process of adjustment where changes occur(ed) across religious and non-religious experiences, generating historiographic, theological and juridical representations of such a diversity.

The three Lectures presented here offer insights on some of the outcomes of this process of adjustment: the role of religious education for today's European society; the challenges faced by academia in understanding change in religion and theology; the chances that religions may offer in supporting agency and resilience for refugees.

Oddrun Bråten, of the Norwegian University of Science and Technology, offered a lecture on *New Social Patterns: Old Educational Structures? Comparative Perspectives on How Diversity Challenges Religious Education in Europe*, describing the issues at stake when religious diversity enters European classrooms and how education can address them. With her lecture, Bråten accepted to combine a review of the last decades of research in Religious Education and diversity from a supranational point of view, and the need to contextualise it to understand its potentialities when it becomes, as a subject, a tool to present, re-present and sustain diversity – in classrooms as well as in larger society.

Religious Education in Europe is one of the fields where the historical predominance of the Christian churches has been progressively challenged, modified and shaped by the outcomes of the process of secularisation, along with migration processes (of Christians and non-Christians), and the re-emergence of religious movements and communities in the public space.

In the past thirty years scholarship tried to grasp these historical dynamics and offer new frameworks, curricula, guidelines to second the ever-emerging diversity in school and university classrooms: Bråten highlights the difficulty in identifying explicit evidence of the possible trajectories following research outcomes in terms of support to decision-making and practice, and her point on the often lacking connection between theories of education, religion and Religious Education offers new tracks for empirical studies, while questing the mechanisms of science-for-policy in such a crucial subject (religious literacy) for present-day and future students.

The former Dean of the Harvard Divinity School, David Hempton, presented, with the lecture *From Nonsectarian to Multireligious: An Educational Experiment in Religious Diversity*, how, from the 1950s on, HDS addressed and embraced religious diversity within its academic programmes and scientific lines of inquiry. Hempton's reconstruction of the debates animating the discussion on the diversification of one of the most globally-recognised centres of excellence in the study of theology and religion offers a reading of the intellectual and cultural history of the United States in those same years. The combination of opportunities offered by changes in the curricula, the changes in leadership and the relevance of money (and the funders behind it) produced a mix of choices, always driven by ideals – and sometimes by ideology, that made HDS a multireligious divinity school. The attention paid to the different layers of diversity, including gender and ethnicity – and its necessary combination with the fairness in access (e.g. to education, technology, employment) are the ingredients which allowed such a transformation in a traditionally-liberal-Protestant institution, which proved able to detect new trends in methodologies and categories for studying religion and explore their potentialities both in terms of student enrolment and in knowledge advancement.

Halina Grzymała-Moszczyńska, president of the International Association for the Psychology of Religion, connected with the EuARe conference to offer an analysis of the work she conducted in 25 years of professional experience with refugees, especially indicating what is the role of faith in helping refugees re-build their lives, identities, stories. With her lecture, *The Role of Religion in Coping with Refugee Trauma: Agency and Resilience* she guides us through the definition of the refugee trauma and points to the many layers of the refugees' identity that should be considered when analysing such a trauma. Grzymała-Moszczyńska reminds us that religion is part of the life of the person who, at a point of his/her life, is also a refugee, and therefore the presence of religion in his/her life should be considered with a more holistic approach. Indeed, religion could be the reason why the refugee flees the country of residence (oppression, persecution), a cage or a bridge during the escape route and towards the communities met in the refugees' dislocation, and a tool offering a meaning for life in unstable conditions and in bridging past and present. What is key for the researcher working with refugees and willing to grasp the role of religion in their lives, is methodology: while quantitative methodology helps in taking pictures of some precise moment of the refugees' life, the qualitative approach makes more room for a deeper understanding of the role religion plays in the refugees' resilience and agency – be it contradictory, linear, supportive, or not.

Finally, among the lecturers was also Madlen Krüger, of the Institute for Interdisciplinary Research in Heidelberg, who presented a lecture on *The Multi-Dimensional Entanglement of Restrictions on Religious Diversity: A Myanmar Case Study*, unfortunately her text could not be included in this volume[1].

The lectures at the 2022 EuARe Annual conference, along with the many panels and papers presented on the topic of "Religion and Diversity" describe diversity as being both a lens for the scholar to read religion and a dimension from which most of the global communities, societies, institutions and decision-makers cannot escape. Indeed, the European Academy of Religion has always been – and will always be - committed to the promotion of diversity: it is the only way for scholarship to flourish and effectively be at the service of society.

---

1 Videos of all EuARe2022 keynote lectures are available on the Youtube Channel of *Fondazione per le scienze religiose*, FscireTV.

Oddrun M. H. Bråten

New Social Patterns: Old Educational Structures? Comparative Perspectives on How Diversity Challenges Religious Education in Europe

Abstract: New social patterns of increased societal diversity when it comes to religions and worldviews have challenged traditional forms of Religious Education (RE) in European school systems. This has led to an increased research interest in religious education and diversity, which is probably the most explored topic in the field of RE, for decades and presently. In this paper, I make an incision into the debates to represent these developments. I will be visiting "classics" such as 'the Interpretive Approach' and 'Signposts' but give special attention to comparative studies. By this I wish to enlighten the debate from a supranational perspective; a perspective transcending the often very intense national debates. Attention will be paid to issues such as the relationship between Church, State and RE in Europe, Human Rights Issues, and education about and into Islam in European states. Lastly, I am also to comment on some recent debates in England; and in Norway, where there is a new national curriculum from 2020. I will keep a focus on the question "what is the role of scholarship" in RE?

Keywords: Religious diversity; religious education; comparative perspectives; church, state and RE in Europe; Islamic Religious Education

1 Introduction

This article is based on a keynote at the European Academy of Religion in Bologna in 2022. An aim was to represent Religious Education (RE) in a context where religion and plurality in general was on the agenda. To give a perspective on the significance of diversity for developments within RE was a tremendous task, because

---

Oddrun M. H. Bråten, Institute of Teacher Education, Norwegian University og Science and Technology, Trondheim, Norway. oddrun.m.braten@ntnu.no
https://orcid.org/0000-0002-3426-0893

Open Access. © 2024 by Oddrun M. H. Bråten, published by De Gruyter. This work is licensed under the Creative under the Creative Commons Attribution 4.0 International License
https://doi.org/10.1515/9783111026176-002

in the field of RE, the issue of increased societal religious diversity has for decades been one of the most discussed topics. To start from a personal perspective, societal religious diversification was the reason why I entered the field, as one of the first in Norway with a religious studies background, at a time when educational policy shifted to one inclusive RE subject for all. The historical background in Norway was a long tradition of Lutheran Christian Education. It was the Reformation that motivated the introduction of schooling for all in 1739. This happened after the Danish king, who ruled Norway at the time, had converted from Catholic to Protestant. Christian Education was for a long time the main aim of general schooling, but over time in the process of the European Enlightenment and other societal developments, education got additional purposes. Today RE in Norway is a small subject among other school subjects, with the purpose of learning about religion, worldviews, philosophy, and ethics.

Between 1974 and 1997 a secular Worldviews school subject existed as an alternative in Norway, though the majority of children had Christian RE. From 1997, after a period of increased religious diversification due to immigration, Norway got one inclusive RE subject for all, in the Norwegian comprehensive centralised educational system.[1] There is a limited right to exemption from activities, not from knowledge content. This has been controversial and a reoccurring topic in political debates. Parental complaints by secular humanists were brought before the European court of Human Rights (ECHR) in Strasbourg, with a verdict against the state of Norway in 2007. The verdict stated that parental rights were not sufficiently respected (Lied 2009). Due to this, the national curriculum and the legislation was adjusted. The name of the subject has shifted with shifting policies, and the present name is *Christianity, Religion, Worldviews and Ethics ("KRLE")*. The specific mention of Christianity in the name, was taken out after the verdict in Strasbourg, but was reinserted when politics shifted to a conservative government in 2013, against strong opposition. Societal debates on RE and school is ongoing in Norway as it is in many European countries today.

Though my own starting point is Norway, I will have a broad European perspective in this article. In the following I will start with a general introduction to the theme *Religious Education and Diversity*, then focus on *Comparative Perspectives*. I include also comments on *Islamic Religious Education (IRE) in Europe*. Towards the end I will comment on some *Recent Developments in England and in*

---

[1] In Norway private alternatives to state schools hardly exist. Very few schools of alternative pedagogy exist, such as Waldorf schools, and a very low number of religiously based schools exists, all of them Christian. In effect more or less all Norwegian pupils have this inclusive RE (Skeie and Bråten 2014, 219–220).

Norway before some *Concluding Remarks*. I will keep a focus on the question "what is the role of scholarship in RE"?[2]

2 Religious Education and Diversity

The situation in Norway back in the second half of the 1990s, was that this new inclusive RE-subject was introduced. Now "all" religions should be taught to all children. In effect, what was taught was five world religions, secular humanism as worldview, and philosophy and ethics (the latter mainly based on Western traditions). In teacher education at the time, most RE teachers had Christian studies or theology background. As one of the first with a religious studies background, my first responsibility was to teach the *'other'* religions. Later, 'othering' in inclusive models became a concern in my own research (Bråten 2013, 202–207). Around the introduction of inclusive RE in Norway, many were looking to England. A similar inclusive subject had developed there, since 1988 in the national legislation, and even before that in local areas because of the system of constructing the syllabi for RE at local levels. Some professionals such as Robert Jackson (University of Warwick) and John Hull (University of Birmingham) were brought over to Norway to enlighten the debate.

The Interpretive Approach (Jackson 1997) is the result of a pioneering work by a team of researchers at the University of Warwick, aimed at solving the challenge posed to RE by increased societal religious diversity. Children and parents had a greater variety of different religious backgrounds than the selection of materials for teaching in school represented. This could mean that a child is taught about his / her "own" tradition, in a way which is alien to him / her - or learns about religion in ways which are not useful for understanding more about their own or other people's religions in the present diverse society. The internal diversity of the grand religious traditions also became obvious as the work by the Warwick team was based on ethnographic studies into the lives of, for instance "Hindu children in Britain" (Jackson and Nesbitt 1993). It gave a certain focus on the "lived" side of religion, which is probably closer to children's experience than tenets of faith, or the history of the traditions which was often the traditional content of school learning. The approach is anthropological in its perspectives / theoretical foundation, but this is

---

[2] This was a challenge posed to me when I was given the assignment of delivering this keynote.

combined with profound pedagogical groundwork that put the child in the centre of the attention.³

Jackson distinguishes between religion as grand *traditions*, *groups* within those traditions, and *individuals*. This pedagogical approach encourages an understanding of religion as dynamic and evolving, countering essentialising representations which can create harmful stereotypes of religions in education, presented as simple fixed entities. There are three main principles to reflect on in teaching religion in a plural context according to the *Interpretive Approach*: *representation*: how a religion is represented, what is selected as the content of teaching and thus forming what students take away from the teaching; *interpretation*: how materials for study is interpreted by students, and *reflexivity*: for students to reflect on that which is presented to them in relation to their own experiences / backgrounds. This would ensure reflecting on the relevance of what is learned, in and for their own lives.

In the project "Bridges to Religion", the Warwick team produced a series of booklets which illustrated this pedagogical idea (e.g., Barrett 1994). Here children in schools studying religion met the major religious traditions (in Britain mainly Judaism, Christianity, Islam, Hinduism, Buddhism and Sikhism) through adherents like themselves in age. The material presents a glimpse of what it is like for children to live in and with their religion. From such an entry students can move to contextualise that experience in relation to that child's immediate relations, such as groups within that religion that the child and his / her family belong to. In this way one gets an alternative route to learning about the grand religious traditions, which puts the children's lived experiences in the centre of attention (Jackson 1997).

The *Interpretive Approach* is possibly the most well-known theory of diversity and RE, and has spurred widespread interest, debate, and controversy. Here I only include one example: Leni Franken revisited the theoretical foundations of it, in an article from 2018 ("Religious Studies and Nonconfessional RE: Countering the Debates"), arguing that the *Interpretive Approach* is a possible way out of ongoing debates about dilemmas of what are neutral grounds for inclusive RE.

"One problem for religious education is that "religions" and "cultures" are rarely presented in a vibrant, flexible, and organic way. RE tends to treat 'religions' as discrete belief systems, and 'cultures' (when they are discussed at all) as separate,

---

3 In Norway Sissel Østberg (1998) and Tove Nicolaisen (2018) have conducted ethnographic research inspired by the work in Warwick. Lars Iversen (2012), Oddrun M. H. Bråten (2013), and many others have been inspired by and have cooperated with Professor Jackson over the years. Especially professor Geir Skeie, whose main interest has been religious education and diversity, has worked closely with him, for instance in the 8 countries EU project "REDCo": Religion in Education. A contribution to Dialogue or a factor of Conflicts in transforming societies of European countries (e.g. Weisse 2010).

bounded entities". Franken (2018) quotes Jackson's book *Religious Education: An Interpretive Approach* (1997, 47).

> The "content" of RE is not simply data provided by the teacher but includes the knowledge and experience of the participants and an interactive relationship between the two. The specialist religious education teacher, working with children from diverse backgrounds, needs the professional skill to manage learning that is dialectical. If teachers can have the right degree of sensitivity towards their students' own positions, as well as to the material studied, and can develop appropriate pedagogies, then a genuinely conversational form of RE can take place which can handle diversity.[4]

We see that here, there is no demand for the teacher to have a particular religious or theological / religious studies background, rather it is a demand for the teacher to have professional skills. With this, Franken claims, dilemmas of "outsiders" vs. "insiders" are countered, through the pedagogical approach.

2.1 The Role of Scholarship: *Signposts* as Example

Regarding the question *"What is the role of scholarship in religious education?"*, it could initially be helpful to make the distinction between *role vis a vis policy* and *role vis a vis educational practice.* Geir Skeie (2017) has found that since the 1990s research in the field of RE in the Nordic countries has had a focus on the complexity of (religious) diversity, including teachers' strategies to handle this. A development in research interest in the Nordic countries had gone from a pedagogical focus on teaching Christianity, in the main, to how to handle societal plurality. Because of this, the scholarly debate on diversity and RE is quite advanced, but this has little impact at the political level, where the focus is rather on whether Christianity has a special role in the country's cultural heritage and thus in society and in education. For instance, in Norway political debates about RE are linked to the school's values clause, which lists certain foundational values seen as rooted in "Christian and Humanistic heritage and tradition". At the same time as maintaining a cultural heritage where Christianity is seen as having a special role, it is also an explicit aim of inclusive RE to contribute to societal integration (see also Iversen 2012). Thus, Norwegian RE could be seen as a train on two tracks, where one is to contribute to integration in the face of increased societal diversity, while another is to maintain a "Christian and Humanist" cultural heritage. The political debate about this subject

---

[4] Franken (2018) quoting Jackson's book *Rethinking Religious Education and Plurality: Issues in Diversity and Pedagogy* (2004, 89).

is however far removed from insights from the body of research and its discussions of the diversity and pedagogy.

Regarding the role of scholarship on a European level, I regard *Signposts – Policy and Practice for Teaching about Religions and Non-Religious Worldviews in Intercultural Education* (Jackson 2014) a substantial effort to bridge the gaps of research and policy, and research and practice. The background was that policy already being agreed on by the countries of the Council of Europe, was not followed up nationally (Jackson 2014, 7–19). Thus, in *Signposts*, Jackson tries to explain it, in a form which is applicable for practical usage. For instance, an important distinction is made between "understanding religion(s)" and "religious understanding" (p. 22), recognizing that outsiders and insiders' perspectives has distinctive qualities. Both may be important for understanding religion(s) as an aspect of own and others culture. Strangely, issues of religion have often been left to one side when *Intercultural Education* has been on the agenda (e.g., Jackson 2014, 21–22). From such a perspective it is also a matter of how religion could be brought into that mix. This is however not to say that that is all that RE could be or, empirically speaking, *is*. This becomes apparent through further mapping of the realities of RE at schools in Europe conducted since then for instance in the book series *Religious Education at schools in Europe* (for each of the six volumes there are different co-editors besides Martin Rothgangel and Martin Jäggle 2015–2020.)

Some main topics in *Signposts* include issues of terminology internationally, religious literacy (p. 27–31), competence and didactics for understanding religions (p. 33–46), the classroom as "safe space" for student-to-student dialogue within the school (p. 47–57), the representation of religion in the media, and also books and other resources (p. 59–65), non-religious convictions and world views (p. 67–75), human rights issues, (p. 77–86), and linking schools to wider communities and organisations, (p. 87–97). On all those topics RE research is cited, and research and debates are also developed further since then. One such development, initiated by Robert Jackson himself, was a special issue of the journal *Intercultural Education*. Dealing with education in plural societies is the focus of the journal, and here perspectives on religious plurality in an intercultural context is allocated a space within the broader debate on plurality and education. In this special issue there is a focus on Inclusive RE, featuring articles like: "The relationship between religious education and intercultural education" (Lund Johannesen & Skeie 2018), "Issues in the integration of religious education and worldviews education in an intercultural context" (Bråten & Everington 2018) and "Qur'anic education and non-confessional RE: an intercultural perspective (Berglund & Gent 2018)".

Has *Signposts* affected *policy* on national levels? To a very limited degree it could seem, according to a recent comment by Martin Rothgangel, in the book *Islamic Religious Education in Europe: A Comparative Study* (Franken and Gent 2021).

I will get back to this in the section about Islam in education below. Has *Signposts* effected *practice?* Despite the effort to bridge the gap, *Signposts* could be seen as aiming for impact on the policy level rather than the level of practice. However, it has been translated to 13 languages, and there are teacher training modules based on it available at the European Wergeland Centre.[5] To the extent that *Signposts* is being read by actors close to practice, like teachers and teacher educators, and they pick up points seen as relevant in their own teaching practice, then the research that this is based on will have an impact. Ideas discussed in *Signposts* may have an impact on practice even if they were not integrated in national policy in a formal way. However, the impact of research on both policy and practice is hard to track, and here more research is needed to be able to answer this with more accuracy. A key point regarding the role of scholarship in education is whether, or to what degree, teachers or even teacher educators read the increasing body of research on RE or have an idea of what insights this body of research represents. A better overview of this body of research could be called for, for instance through more reviews. Strengthening of education for RE teachers would also be important.

3 Comparative Perspectives

When I came into the field of Religious Education, at a time of shift to an inclusive model in Norway, many were looking to England for inspiration. I think two main things caused me to do a PhD with Robert Jackson at the University of Warwick: 1. When I encountered the *Interpretive Approach* it gave me directions regarding how to proceed with teaching in the new inclusive RE subject in Norway, and 2. I wanted to understand the English context where some impulses came from. It soon became apparent that I was going to do a comparative study of RE in England and Norway, but it was not apparent how. In the process, the *methodology* developed in order to conduct the study, became a main point, visualised in the title of the book: *Towards a Methodology for Comparative Studies in Religious Education: A Study of England and Norway* (Bråten 2013). The core of the methodology and example of main findings in my original study is presented in the article 'Three dimensions and four levels: towards a methodology for comparative religious education' (Bråten 2015).

---

5 *Signposts teacher training module, Teaching about religions and non-religious world views in intercultural education* – The European Wergeland Centre (https://theewc.org/resources/signposts-teacher-training-module-teaching-about-religions-and-non-religious-world-views-in-intercultural-education/[accessed on March 25, 2024]).

The background for the suggested methodology was multidisciplinary, collecting perspectives from comparative education, comparative religious studies, and pioneering works in comparative RE (Bråten 2013, 29–55). One point in my conceptualisation of comparative studies here, is that it is about the study of internationally shared problems and how they affect different (national) contexts. It is to have *a supranational perspective*, meaning a view transcending the often very intense national debates. The idea to focus on the impact of internationally shared problems on national processes is acquired from comparative education. The methodology is analytic rather than purely descriptive, aiming at comparative analysis. I claim it is suited to explain variations across national cases and have tried to demonstrate this point further in later publications.

I argue that three dimensions should be considered in comparative studies: *supranational, national,* and *subnational processes*, which is one of two core ideas of this methodology. The methodology is illustrated by this model:

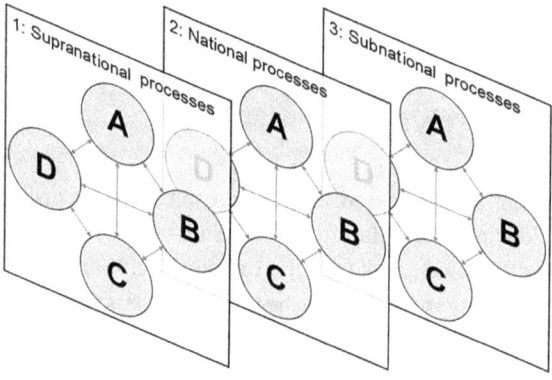

Fig. 1: Model of the three dimensions and four levels methodology

Here we see these three dimensions, and they are conceptualized as processes. These are processes which are seen to potentially affect RE teaching and learning. This is combined with four levels, which is really 'levels of curriculum', an idea gained from Jon Goodlads theories of curricula (e.g. Goodlad & Su 1992). In this model there is:

A. a societal level (perceptions and debates in the society, including research)
B. an institutional level (formal written curricula)
C. an instructional level (teaching)
D. an experiential level (students learnings and experiences)

The levels are included to secure stronger validity in comparative studies through thoroughness in exploring national history and local school systems - and acknowledging the complexity of 'curriculum'. I have argued that together the dimensions and the levels make up a map of domains of relevance for teaching and learning in RE. As such it is also suitable for finding new research questions, for instance of relationships between domains (Bråten 2016, 46).[6] I distinguish also between *formal and informal processes*, where for example verdicts in the European court of Human Rights are examples of a *formal* supranational process. In Norway such a verdict affected national formal curriculum in 2007/8 (Lied 2009). Societal changes of the population's relationship to religion(s) and worldviews locally, nationally, and internationally, for instance through processes of globalisation and mediatisation, would be examples of *informal* processes.

Finally, I want to draw attention to the arrows in the model: illustrating how this is not a top-down model of how policy effects practice but is rather meant to illustrate how impulses can go either way. For instance, it was the increased numbers of immigrant children in Birmingham UK, which spurred John Hulls, famous 1975 innovative interreligious Birmingham agreed syllabus (Birmingham 1975). I call these impulses *'bypasses'* (Bråten 2013, 193, see also Korsvoll 2021).[7] Impulses from *Signposts* on teaching in national / local contexts, even when the national policy does not reflect those ideas, would also be examples of *bypasses*. In this case impulses from international policy and research are bypassing the formal level of curriculum, into practice, and thus impact practice despite perhaps not having impacted policy.

---

[6] Questions about relationships between domains could for instance be, what is the student's relationship to societal debates on RE? What is the relationship between the formal written curriculum and what / how teachers teach? What is the relationship between education at a local level and debates about RE at a national, or even supranational level? For example: in a small village in Lofoten, Norway, the local school suddenly has a number of Catholic students, as their parents have migrated from Poland to work in the fishing industry. Does the local teacher imagine Polish Catholicism as part of the context when she teaches about Christianity?

[7] Lately Korsvoll (2021) has identified a bypass in an analysis of how textbook authors in Norway emphasised plurality and tolerance more than could be expected based on the formal Norwegian National Curriculum for RE. While in the formal curriculum ideas of Christian and humanist national heritage were emphasised more, in the textbooks the focus was on integrative perspectives with regard to increased societal worldviews diversity.

3.1 New Social Patterns: Old Educational Structures, Comparative Perspectives on How Diversity Challenges Religious Education in Europe

The book series *Religious Education at Schools in Europe* maps RE in all European countries. Each nation report is arranged in 12 categories, providing a source of amazing overviews of the situation for RE in Europe, and an ideal material for further comparative analysis.[8] For Part 2: Western Europe I was challenged to give a comparative perspective of aspects of RE in those countries represented in the volume: Belgium, the Netherlands, France, Luxembourg, Scotland, the Republic of Ireland, Northern Ireland, Wales, and England.

In the analysis, I utilized the three dimensions and four levels methodology. I called this chapter *"New Social Patterns: Old Structures? How the Countries of Western Europe Deal with Religious Plurality in Europe."* This title reflected the results of the analysis. In this article I considered the traditional religious landscapes, the societal plurality in those countries consisted of at the time, and current conceptions and tasks of RE. While striking differences in conceptions and tasks for RE were apparent, challenges discussed in all chapters related to increased religious diversity. Yet, the way that these challenges are dealt with in each setting, was very different.

I found four main approaches to dealing with religious diversity *in educational systems* (p. 305, see also Bråten 2016, 44):

1. To maintain a religiously plural educational system (e.g. Belgium: private religious schools dominate)
2. To promote a common educational system with inclusive RE (e.g. Scotland)
3. In the face of secularity, education strictly about religious facts (France)
4. Parallel subject options (e.g. in State schools in Belgium)

It becomes clear that there is often more than one way of dealing with religious plurality in one country, for instance between private and state schools, or between

---

[8] In addition to the chapter *"New social patterns: old structures? How the countries of Western Europe deal with religious plurality in Europe"* (Bråten 2014b) which I will elaborate on below, I also contributed to the chapter "Religious Education at Schools in Norway" (Skeie and Bråten 2014), and to an introductory chapter to Part 3: Northern Europe, named "Are Oranges the only fruits: A discussion of comparative studies in Religious Education in relation to the plural nature of the field internationally" (Bråten 2014a). An issue here is whether REs across Europe are so different that comparisons make any sense, but despite apparent huge differences and conceptual confusions between languages, I argue to the contrary, that comparative efforts create new insights, and a new possibility to reflect on one's own home context (Bråten 2014a).

regions of independent educational systems within a country (sub national dimension in the model above). The kind of responses to religious diversity that existed, depended heavily on national religious- and school history, or "the tale thereof" (see 'national imaginary' as explained below). In the tale of the history of the nation, religion is often allocated a specific role, and this history is described as "deep", cultural and intersecting with the identity of the nation. A quote from the chapter on Belgium illustrates this point:

> Religious Education in Belgium, in the public realm of the school, is dealing with this broader European and global diversity, but because of the small space of the country and its deep history, the discourses on religious education seem to be even more intense. (Derroitte et al. 2014, 57)

Thus, a pattern of "same but different" came to the fore, that the state / school / religion relationship in history, or the tale of it, seemed determent for what possibilities were available presently in each national context, to address societal diversity. This left me pondering for several reasons, but among other things because, even if the task of writing this chapter had expanded my own views, this finding was based on one chapter from each of those countries, while the England-Norway comparison conducted earlier was much more thorough about national contexts. To explore the matter further, I called a symposium at NCRE in Trondheim (2019) and the result became a Special Issue (SI) of *Religion & Education* (Vol. 48(3)), published in 2021. Here scholars with previous experience of comparative studies explored the question of *how religion in different contexts, including history, impacts (religious) education systems*. Attention to methodology for comparative studies is also followed up in this issue.

In my original study (Bråten 2013, 113) I had found that specific similarities between English and Norwegian RE were somewhat incidental. Pluralisation of society is put forward as a reason for change to inclusive models in both countries, but whether changes could happen seemed to depend on nation-specific factors, particularly the history of church, state and religion, or *the tale thereof*. This is why a combined focus on the supranational and the national is necessary. Why did changes to inclusive models happen in some places but not others where societal diversity is no less?

My work with the article *"New Social Patterns: Old Structures?* (Bråten 2014b) had revealed a pattern of increased religious diversity in the population (documented by statistics sited in the books chapters), and school systems and forms of RE that seemed to be resisting adjusting to those changes. In the introduction to the special issue I therefore present this as *a hypothesis* for further exploration: *that new social patterns reflecting the present plurality are not sufficiently accounted for in educational systems, as they rather reflect the traditional religious landscapes.* This is explored in the articles in the issue, and in the following I will include some comments based on some of them.[9]

In "The Role of Space and Time: A Comparative Exploration of Religion and Education, Introduction to the Special Issue" (Bråten 2021b), I elaborate on the concept *"national imaginary"*, which is also discussed in my original comparative work (Bråten 2013, 115–118). When history is described as 'deep' and connected to religion, identity, culture, I have used the idea of 'national imaginary' to describe this (Schiffauer et al. 2004, 4–8), and to catch the fact that the idea of history is not identical to what really happened. It is 'the tale of' the history of the nation rather than what happened. Benedict Anderson (1983) has described 'imagined communities', and Charles Taylor refers to this when he writes about 'modern social imaginaries' (Taylor 2004). A country's religious history is often very particular and related to the idea of the nation. In the process of enlightenment, belonging to modern nations became bundled together with religions in different ways. However, during the second half of the 20th century religion and national identity has become unbundled for a significant amount of people (Andersland 2021, 61–62).

For instance, today, for Islamic Norwegians, nationality is not relevant for religious identity. For others living in that same country however, it is relevant, but in the face of the pluralisation it becomes important to negotiate new ways of integrating religious and national identity, for instance through a rhetoric that all share in the Christian cultural heritage, if not the Christian faith. I believe this bundling and unbundling of religion and nation becomes particularly visible when looking at debates about RE in national school systems.

---

[9] Short note on articles in the SI which is not elaborated below: Doney, J. (2021) "Unearthing Ecumenical Influences on Educational Policy in England and Norway using Statement Archology": is about "digging out" how something becomes possible, here focusing on the Christian Ecumenical movement as a supranational process that made inclusive RE possible – in England and Norway. It illustrates how history affected what happened, but also what might happen today. In Eastern Europe, inclusive RE did not so far become possible, typically RE is catechetical. In "The RE-Puzzle of the Visegrád-Group and the Answer of 'Collective Memory'" Rothgangel, M. (2021b) compares RE in Poland, Czech Republic, Slovakia, and Hungary, which share a history of being part of the Habsburg empire, by using theory of collective memory. He thus explores some other kinds of "structures" in addition to state and church relationships. In Miedema (2021) "A Postlude on Adequate Methodologies for Comparative Research Regarding the Relation of Religion / Worldview and Education", he notes how articles even in this issue reflect a longstanding strong focus on context in RE-research. He refers to Skeie (2013, 249–272) who has noted a "contextual turn" in research on religion and education, that we have "seen in religious education research an increasing emphasis on the relationship between objects of study and their social and cultural surroundings, and this has been discussed not only as a methodological, but also as an epistemological issue".

In "Church, State and RE in Europe: Past, Present, Future" Leni Franken (2021) explains why some "structures" are so hard to change: both religion and schooling are frequently integrated into nations' constitutions. As a background for the legislation one can find conflicts from the past, laid to a form of rest. Real structural shifts to models more suitable to the new situation with increased societal diversity therefore require constitutional amendments. Since there is often no political will to do so, the gap to "worldviews realities" among the student population widens. In this situation, teachings in school can be perceived to be irrelevant by the students and parents. Franken even finds that sometimes *pragmatic shifts* happen with "creative interpretations of constitutions" as teachers and schools experience the problem as quite pressing (Franken 2021, 428).

In this article a finding is also that shifts to integrative models have been easier in countries where the church has historically been a state actor. This kind of inclusive RE seems to have become possible in those nations that were historically Protestant, such as the Nordic countries, England, Wales, and Scotland. In cases of stricter separation between states and religion, typically in traditionally Catholic countries in southern parts of Europe, shifts to integrative models have (largely) not become possible. For instance, in Belgium, this means a large percentage of the schools are private and Catholic with forms of catholic RE (though sometimes described as "open"). At the same time there is an amazingly plural / secular population if you look at the statistics. Thus, provision in school is far removed from the realities of students and parents' real worldviews, but because of the historical and political significance of, in this case, the Catholic Church, in national and school history, there is little political will for changes of the constitution on this point.[10] In a sense this finding has some similarities with Skeie's (2017) findings regarding the Nordic countries, despite entirely different school systems and RE there, with a Protestant history and an integrative form of RE, in the sense that even here there is a gap between RE-research and RE-policy. In both national cases we apparently see a conflict between pedagogical intent to teach in a way relevant to students, and to suite political aims having to do with historical and juridical relations between religion, state, and school. School and education are very politicised issues, and no less so when the subject at hand is religion. There is a danger that RE becomes a means not so much for children's learning, as for different political agendas.

The pragmatic solutions Franken reveals, showcase the gap between pedagogies to adjust to societal realities, and formal structures of education. It seems that "traditional religion" is holding its grounds, both in integrative and separative

---

10 Still, with intense societal debates changes are also happening in many countries, and even in Belgium, as is also documented in this article.

forms of RE. In integrated models, as for instance in Norway, it is still Christianity in the main, often with reference to its importance as cultural heritage. A problem with this approach is also that Christianity is represented as "Norwegian" rather than global, so that the Christian diversity, which is a reality in Norway today, is not well represented either. In effect, neither for instance Islam nor the often-privileged Christian faith(s) are taught as living, negotiated, present and global religions, which students in today's plural, globalised media reality meet.

Considering the discrepancy between existing educational systems and societal developments, how are these systems justified? As it turned out, in "New Social Patterns, Old Structures", ensuring Human Rights was central in all these country models. Ensuring Human Rights was used as an argument for justifying almost diametrically opposite systems (as for instance in Belgium vs. France, Bråten 2014b, 304). This is interesting also because, as we know, several cases concerning RE have been brought before ECtHR, and these court cases bring attention to the situation for religious *minorities*. In "The Effects of Judgements by the European Court of Human Rights on Religious Education in England and Turkey" by Abdurrahman Hendek and Nigel Fancourt (2021), they find that such verdicts are used selectively by politicians of different nations, to justify their own politics. In their article they see how England having no verdicts against them, while Turkey has two, is a major difference in how important such international jurisprudence becomes in the national debates. In so doing they explore the relationship between national debates and politics and the formal supranational processes in ECtHR. While all nations are in principle bound by the same principles and verdicts, the effects and use of them in national politics varies greatly.

Increased diversity of worldview is not only about religious worldviews. There is also a significant increase of people identifying as 'not religious' (Jackson 2014, 67–75, Bråten 2014b, 291). Paralleled to processes of *pluralisation*, there is also a process of *secularisation* – but what does that mean? Research into the worldviews of those claiming to have "no religion" reveal 'nones' to hold very different views, that may or may not be of a spiritual nature (Lee 2015). They may reject or be unfamiliar with traditional religion. Sometimes the religion – secular divide no longer makes sense, so that their worldviews could be described as non-binary (Bråten 2021). In France we find an elaborated debate on the meaning of secular, but how context sensitive are ideas about "secular"? For instance in Eastern Europe it might be associated with a communist past, whereas this is not the case in Norway, where "secular" could be seen as 'neutral'. In his article "Comparing Through Contrast: Reshaping Incongruence into a Mirror", Kristian Niemi (2021) explores how important context is for the meaning of concepts like "secular" and "religion". He describes how "secular" in India is nothing like "secular" in Sweden. That his research questions were framed from a Swedish idea of "secular" and "religious", caused the "friction" when studying RE in India. Through the act of comparing and exploring the "friction", he gains new views on Sweden (Niemi 2021, 470).

An example of "friction" is when his Swedish ideas of what "secular" is and what "religious" is, appear as coloured by a Christian Protestant view, in the sense that his understanding of "religion" was primarily understood as *"belief" / words*, whereas in India religion is often translated to dharma, meaning *"duties" / actions*. Niemi's article is a development of methodology as well, introducing the idea of "mirroring", and the concepts "comparandum" (the frame), "comparatum" (mirror glass).

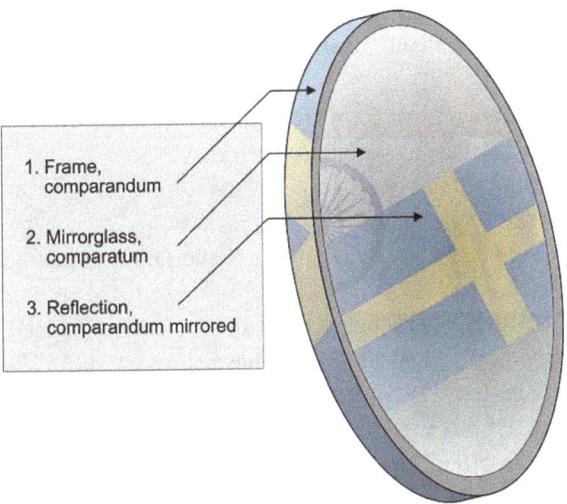

Fig. 2: Model illustrating Niemi's ideas of 'mirroring" (Niemi 2021, 470)

Through the act of comparing and exploring the 'friction', here meaning lack of similar meaning of core concepts (secular / religion), in the reflection he gains new perspectives on Sweden. The effort to compare RE despite the friction, can even be said to contribute to the larger debates of the meaning of such core concepts in religious studies as such. In using India as a "comparatum" he makes visible an Eurocentrism, in the way 'secular' and 'religious' is understood in Swedish RE.

3.2 Islamic Religious Education (IRE) in Europe

I will comment on Islam based on a recent publication: *Islamic Religious Education in Europe: A Comparative Study* (Franken & Gent 2021). The background for this initiative, was the increased number of Muslim students in schools across Europe, and increasing attention for Islamic RE, not the least in the perspective of discourses of radicalisation, politisation and securitisation. One question is what the relationship is between what states / society expect from (I)RE, and what Muslim communities expect.

By initiating an anthology with a comparative perspective, Franken and Gent create an overview of *forms of* and *embeddedness for* IRE across Europe. The book contains 14 country reports. The selection is countries where Muslims are a significant minority, with some exceptions such as Cyprus where in parts there is a Muslim majority. In addition, there is a commentary section with short chapters on topics such as "Postcolonial and Feminist Perspectives in Islamic Religious Education" (Marianne Hafnor Bø) and "Teaching about Islam: Insights from Hermeneutics" (Farid Panjwani).

Four main forms of embeddedness for IRE are identified:
- IRE (education into), in state schools (e.g. Belgium, Austria)
- Education *about* Islam, in state schools (e.g. Sweden, Norway)
- IRE in Islamic schools (e.g. the Netherlands, France)
- RE in confessional (Christian) schools (e.g. Belgium, the Netherlands, Germany)

Through focusing on Islamic RE some general points regarding RE are enlightened, at the same time as Islam specifically gets some much-needed attention. In the words from Hendek (2021) book review, *"The fate of RE determines the fate of IRE in a country"*: a point which could not be caught without a comparative perspective. In my short chapter I compare, in brief, IRE in Cyprus, the Netherlands and Denmark based on the country reports. The comparison illustrated quite clearly how the national contexts determines what kind of IRE there is: if Christian RE is confessional, IRE (and other kinds of REs) is confessional; if the history is of strict separation of state and religion, there is no RE, and thus no IRE in state schools (such as in France), and it seems it was in areas where traditionally Protestant state churches dominated, where inclusive RE developed, through the terms of the inclusiveness is also an issue. Here we now find IRE as teaching about rather than into Islam, as part of inclusive RE subjects.

What we can actually claim to see in a comparative perspective, is how parts of European history that regulated Christianity / Christian RE through historical bickering back and forth between Christian religions and European states, created a certain deal for Christian Education specific to each state / nation (see also Franken 2021). In each case this deal for Christian RE is expanded to "other" religions, such as Islam. A question is, however, how well that fits? Maybe the deal for teaching about or into forms of Christian religion, needs to be renegotiated to fit Islam specifically. The history of Christianity and Islam in Europe are very different, and yet Islam could also be seen to be a part of European cultural heritage. The comparative perspectives in the mentioned *Islamic Religious Education in Europe: A Comparative Study* brings into light the terms and conditions for Islam in education in Europe and contributes to a better foundation for discussing how to improve the situation. A general point may be that *more of Europe's history of different religions needs to be written into, and negotiated vis a vis, the story of the nations and it's alleged "deep history", in effect: European "cultural heritage"*. Other than Christian religions such as Islam or Judaism also have a long history of presence in Europe, with their own specific features.

Rothgangel's (2021a) comment "Islamic Religious Education in Europe and European Recommendations as a Mutual Challenge" is relevant for the question of the role of scholarship on policy and practice. In advice such as *Signposts* from the Council of Europe (Jackson 2014), and the Toledo guidelines (from Organization for Security and Co-operation in Europe (OSCE) 2007) the positive value of teachings that respect everyone's right to freedom of religions and beliefs, and teaching that counter stereotypes and prejudice, is stressed. However, Rothgangel observes that almost no reference to this is made in any of the chapters of *Islamic Religious Education in Europe: A Comparative Study* (Franken & Gent 2021). While in the named recommendations religion is seen as a cultural phenomenon that there should be teaching *about*, for integrative purposes, to promote tolerance and societal coherence, this is often not the understanding of the organisers of IRE. He lists several possible reasons for this, but one is that in the often quite hostile societal debate, Muslim pupils feel vulnerable and in need for a "safe space" away from prejudice and discrimination, for instance among peers in Muslim schools. This increases *segregation* at the cost of dialogue and *integration*. Further, the mere complexity of different national contexts where this advice is interpreted (or ignored?), is named as a challenge. How well does the advice fit? This strengthens the view that attention to context is needed.

4 Recent Developments in England and Norway

In England there has for several years now been a murmur of "crisis" (e.g. Conroy et al 2013). A commission of Religious Education has investigated this issue, and in their Final Report from 2018, a way forwards is suggested (CoRE 2018). But the debate continues, and this crisis is on the agenda in Biesta & Hannam's (eds.) book from 2021: *The Forgotten Dimension of Religious Education*.

In my reading I find that according to this book, a forgotten dimension is perspectives on religions as "lived", what it entails to live meaningfully with religion.

However, a main point is how the dimension of religion is lacking in theories of education, while at the same time theories of education are lacking in theories of RE. This is relevant for political argument of justifications for having RE as a subject in schools if there is little agreement over REs nature or purpose. If this crisis is not solved, there is a danger that it will be taken out of the school curriculum. This is, I believe, part of the debate in England presently. For Hannam (chapter 9) a main point of both *Education* and *Religious Education* seems to enable young people to act in a diverse reality, through *subjectification*. This refers to Biesta's theories of education where he distinguishes between *qualification, socialisation, and subjectification*. According to Biesta (chapter 8, 11), subjectification "concerns the ways in which education contributes to the formation of the student as a person – not as an object we try to influence from the outside, so to speak, but as subject in their own right".

In chapter 6 where Gert Biesta interviews Farid Panjwani and Lynn Revel (Biesta, Panjwani and Revell 2021), the focus is *essentialism*, where Islam works as the perfect example of why this is problematic: in the current political climate we find essentialised ideas of what Islam 'really' is. For instance, is Islam compatible with democratic values (or 'British Values')? It is not possible to answer this question fairly with a yes or a no, because Muslims shape Islam and Islam shapes Muslims: Islam is not a static phenomenon, but diverse, context sensitive and evolving, as are also other religions. And still in schools, such questions may be posed to pupils. For instance, we can find such essentialised ideas of religions in textbooks used for children in school. We see how well-educated RE teachers would be important.

Joyce Miller was part of the Commission on Religious Education (CoRE), that worked on the alleged crisis. In "Reflection on the Seminar on Religion and Education: The Forgotten Dimensions of Religions Education" (Miller 2021), chapter 10 in *The Forgotten Dimension of Religious Education* (Biesta and Hannam 2021), Miller reports that while she was doing investigation for the commission, she did observe a lot of what she regarded good quality teaching, but the problem was the lack of coherence to educational structures that supported it. This could be seen to be part of the same tendency that I identified internationally, in "New Social Patterns: Old Structures" (Bråten 2014b). What she asks for are structures that support more open exploration of religion (and worldviews) as phenomena, including as lived realities in people's lives.

Does the alleged crisis in English RE apply elsewhere, for instance in Norway? That would depend on whether teaching of (world) religions as separate entities continue, with essentialising representation of religions as grand unified and monolithic traditions, *or*, whether a kind of teaching could be facilitated *where open exploration of religion and worldviews can happen:* in a way which is seen as meaningful for students: and meaningful in the wider context of the purpose of *education*. A recent suggestion towards such ends in the English context is found in the article "Worldviews and Big Ideas: A Way Forward for Religious Education?" (Freathy & John 2019b).

With regards to a new national curriculum in Norway, which was implemented from 2020, a general point is that subject learning should be meaningful in relation to overarching aims for education. This is specified in three interdisciplinary topics: public health and mastery of life, democracy and citizenship, and sustainable development. These interdisciplinary topics towards which all subjects should contribute, again resonates with more general formulations about the purpose of education as such, in the legislation and general descriptions in this national curriculum. The new National Curriculum also encourages a more open approach to knowledge, in all school subjects, where students are meant to explore issues, and not just learn prefabricated facts. This kind of learning is in policy documents in Norway called deep learning (or in-depth learning) (Bråten and Skeie 2020).

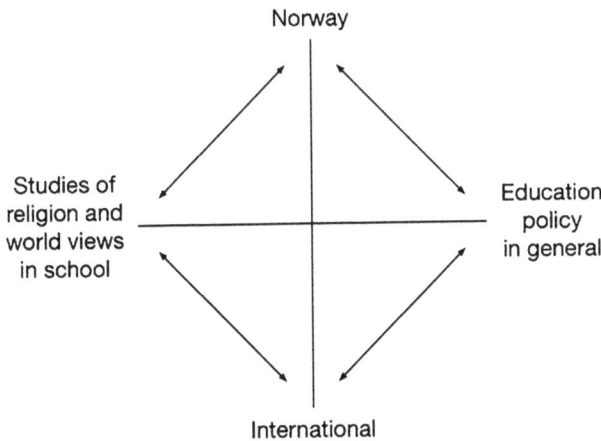

Fig. 3: Dynamics of general and subject specific education policy in an international perspective

The dynamics of educational policy in general and for studies of religion and worldviews in schools specifically, is illustrated in this model (Bråten and Skeie 2020): the model has a general education and specific subject axes, but also a national – international axes. Both educational policy in general and specific to RE, are subject to international trends and exchange of ideas, in formal as well as in informal processes. The model illustrates how specific school subjects are imbedded in the wider context of education. In the history of the inclusive RE subject in Norway since 1997, the curriculum for RE has been changed more frequently than the general National Curriculum (other school subjects), due to societal and juridical conflicts regarding this subject.[11] However, in the current reform, where the National Curriculum for school is renewed in all subjects, it is particularly obvious how general educational ideas affect developments in RE as a school subject.

A new element is for instance how all subjects should contribute towards the three interdisciplinary topics. Further, according to descriptions of the competences that students in schools should acquire through education in the Norwegian public school, students should understand and be able to use what is learned in new situations. Deep learning is described as follows:

> School must provide room for in-depth learning so that the pupils develop understanding of key elements and relationships in a subject, and so they can learn to apply subject knowledge and skills in familiar and unfamiliar contexts. (...). In-depth learning implies applying knowledge and skills in different ways so that over time the pupils will be able to master various types of challenges in the subject, individually and in interaction with others. (Bråten & Skeie 2020, 8).

For each school subject, *key elements* are replacing detailed lists of learning content, and for RE those key elements are:
1. Knowledge of religions and worldviews
2. Exploring religions and worldviews with different methods
3. Exploring existential questions and answers
4. Being able to take another's view
5. Ethical reflections

Together with Geir Skeie (Bråten and Skeie 2020) I argue that because studies of religion and worldviews in school have a lot to contribute to the three interdisciplinary topics, RE in Norway could be seen as strengthened. It has acquired new specific purposes to contribute within the larger framework for general education. Maybe with this curriculum, where the educational purpose of RE is made clearer, a "crisis" of the sort discussed in the English scene, can be avoided? For instance, more open exploration of religion and worldviews can happen in school education, when one of the core elements of the RE curriculum currently reads "exploring religions and worldviews with different methods"? However, that would depend on what happens with it, in teachers and schools' interpretations, and at the instructional and experiential level of education (see also Figure 1: Model of the three dimensions and four levels methodology).

---

[11] General reviews happened in 1997, 2006, 2020, additionally specifically for RE there were also changes, in 2002, 2005, 2016 (Bråten and Skeie 2020).

5 Concluding Remarks

In this presentation I have given an incision into the topic of *Religious Education and diversity*, with a focus on comparative perspectives and included also comments on Islam and Education. Towards the end I commented on some recent developments in England and in Norway. I have kept the question of the role of scholarship in RE in mind. I hope in this article to have demonstrated that scholarship on RE has produced valuable insights and thus may be seen to contribute to bringing issues of religious education and diversity forwards. At the same time, I have also given examples to show that the relationship between research, policy and practice is complicated. The model of the three dimensions and four levels methodology (Figure 1), and the model of Dynamics of general and subject specific education policy in an international perspective (Figure 3) both illustrate this point.

A key point regarding the role of scholarship is, whether or to what degree teachers or teacher educators can access the ever-increasing body of research in RE. A better overview of this research could be called for, for instance through more reviews, but strengthening of education for RE teachers could also be seen as important. We have seen how impulses from *Signposts* on teaching in national / local contexts could influence teaching practices, even when the national policy does not reflect the research-based ideas expressed there through bypasses. On a political level, we have seen how historical bundling and unbundling of religion and nations complicates matters, and how certain aspects of religion and society become particularly visible when looking at debates about RE in national school systems. Here RE research becomes relevant also for the wider studies of religious diversity in society. The effort in research to compare RE despite the 'friction', can be said to contribute to the larger debates of the meaning of core concepts in religious studies as such. For instance, in using India as a "comparatum" Niemi (2021) makes visible an Eurocentrism, in the way 'secular' and 'religious' is understood in Swedish RE.

The comparative perspectives in *Islamic Religious Education in Europe: A Comparative Study* (Franken & Gent 2021) brings into light the terms and conditions for Islam and other religions in Education in Europe. The significance of that is to get a better foundation for discussing how to improve the situation, which could be seen as much needed. A general point here is that: *more of Europe's history of different religions needs to be written into, and negotiated vis a vis, the story of the nations and its alleged "deep history", in effect: European "cultural heritage".*

What do we know about what Religious Education (or Religion and Worldviews Education) is, in a comparative perspective? Some suggestions:
- School subjects (with various names, aims and purposes at national levels)
- *The* purpose of Education? (as it once was in Norway)

- Education *into* faith / membership / a specific religious identity
- Education *about* religions and worldviews in today's world
- Learning *from* religions, worldviews, ethics, and philosophies
- A *means to increased tolerance* and understanding between people
- A means to understand oneself, the world, and "others"
- A *safe space* for dialogue on such issues as religion and worldviews, existential and ethical question
- An opportunity for learning *how* phenomena like religions and worldviews in the world can be studied with different methods (Freathy & John 2019a, Aukland 2021)
- An opportunity to study / explore *how* religious / secular / non-binary worldviews are formed in today's world, and in history (Bråten 2021a)

Empirically speaking, RE is probably all of the above – and more. The role of scholarship in the field of RE could perhaps be framed as "contributing to developments of policy and practice", but also to develop new insights in RE as a field of research. For many working with RE research a main aim is the development of student's understanding of their own and others' religion and worldviews in the world today. Noting the complexity of contexts and embeddedness for such teaching and learnings internationally, in combination with the urgency to improve understanding of one's own and others' religion and worldviews in a complex world, this could be seen as an aim in both secular and religious frameworks, though such different context of course also impacts how this is done. Debates about what is good quality RE continues to be context sensitive.

I would like to argue that RE is not merely an area of applied science, but rather a separate field of research, though connected to other kinds of studies of religion. As "School" is a relevant field for studying religion and worldviews in today's world, RE scholarship should also be seen as contributing to debates on major issues, even such as "what is religion", "what does secular mean", and thus to the broader debate on diversity and religion.

References

Andersland, Inge. 2021. *Religion Education in Politics. Analysis of Ideas in Parliamentary Debates in Norway*. Religious Diversity and Education in Europe, 45. Münster: Waxmann.

Aukland, Knut. 2021. "Å lære hvordan: Forslag til et nytt mål utover å lære om og av religion". In *Nordidactica*, Vol. 11(1): 103–121.

Barrett, Margaret. 1994. *An Egg for Babcha*, Bridges to Religion Series, The Warwick RE Project, Oxford: Heinemann.

Berglund, Jenny, and Bill Gent. 2018. "Qur'anic Education and Non-Confessional RE: An Intercultural Perspective". In *Intercultural Education*, Vol. 30(3): 323–324.

Biesta, Gert and Patricia Hannam (eds.). 2021. *The Forgotten Dimension of Religious Education?* Leiden / Boston: Brill / Sense.

Biesta, Gert, Farid Panjwani and Lynn Revell. 2021. "Teaching about Islam: From Essentialism to Hermeneutics: An Interview with Farid Panjwani and Lynn Revell, by Giert Biesta". In *The Forgotten Dimension of Religious Education?* Edited by Gert Biesta and Patricia Hannam. Leiden / Boston: Brill / Sense, 85–98.

Bråten, Oddrun Marie Hovde. 2013. *Towards a Methodology for Comparative Studies in Religious Education. A Study of England and Norway*. Religious Diversity and Education in Europe, 24. Münster: Waxmann.

Bråten, Oddrun Marie Hovde. 2014a. "Are Oranges the Only Fruit? A Discussion of Comparative Studies in Religious Education in Relation to the Plural Nature of the Field Internationally." In *Religious Education at Schools in Europe. Volume 2: Northern Europe*. Edited by Martin Rothgangel, Geir Skeie, and Martin Jäggle. Göttingen: Vandenhoeck & Ruprecht.

Bråten, Oddrun Marie Hovde. 2014b. "New Social Patterns: Old Structures? How the Countries of Western Europe Deal with Religious Plurality in Education?" In *Religious Education at Schools in Europe. Volume 2: Western Europe*. Edited by Martin Rothgangel, Robert Jackson, and Martin Jäggle. Göttingen: Vandenhoeck & Ruprecht.

Bråten, Oddrun Marie Hovde. 2015. "Three Dimensions and Four Levels: Towards a Methodology for Comparative Religious Education". *British Journal of Religious Education*, Vol. 37(2): 138–152.

Bråten, Oddrun Marie Hovde. 2016. "Comparative Studies in Religious Education: Perspectives Formed around a Suggested Methodology". In *Religious Education in a Global-Local World*. Edited by Jenny Berglund, Yafa Shanneik, and Brian Bocking. Boundaries of Religious Freedom, 4. Switzerland: Springer.

Bråten, Oddrun Marie Hovde, and Judith Everington. 2018. "Issues in the Integration of Religious Education and Worldviews Education in an intercultural Context." In *Intercultural Education*, Vol. 30(3): 289–305.

Bråten, Oddrun Marie Hovde and Geir Skeie. 2020. "'Deep Learning' in Studies of Religion and Worldviews in Norwegian Schools? The Implications of the National Curriculum Renewal in 2020". In *Religions* 11(11): 579.

Bråten, Oddrun Marie Hovde. 2021a. "Non-Binary Worldviews in Education". In *British Journal of Religious Education*, Vol. 44(3): 325–335.

Bråten, Oddrun Marie Hovde. 2021b. "The Role of Space and Time. A Comparative Exploration of Religion and Education, Introduction to the Special Issue." In *Religion & Education*, Vol. 48(4): 367 383.

Conroy, James C., David Lundie, Robert A. Davis, Vivienne Baumfield, Philip Barnes, Tony Gallagher, Kevin Lowden, Nicole Bourque, and Karen J. Wenell. 2013. *Does Religious Education Work?* London: Bloomsbury.

CoRE (Commission on Religious Education). 2018. *Final Report: Religion and Worldviews: The Way Forwards. A National Plan*. London: Religious Education Council of England & Wales.

Doney, Jonathan. 2021. "Unearthing Ecumenical Influences on Education Policy in England and Norway using Statement Archaeology". In *Religion & Education*, Vol. 48(4): 384–396.

Franken, Leni. 2021. "Church, State and RE in Europe: Past, Present and Future". In *Religion & Education*, Vol 48(4): 417–435.

Franken, Leni. 2018. "Religious Studies and Nonconfessional RE: Countering the Debates", *Religion & Education*, Vol. 45(2): 155–172.

Franken, Leni and Bill Gent. 2021. *Islamic Religious Education in Europe: A Comparative Study.* Routledge Research in Religion and Education, 8. London: Routledge.

Freathy, Rob, and Helen C. John. 2019a. "Religious Education, Big Ideas and the Study of Religion(s) and Worldview(s)". In *British Journal of Religious Education*, Vol. 41(1): 27–40.

Freathy, Rob, and Helen C. John. 2019b. "Worldviews and Big Ideas: A Way Forward for Religious Education?" In: *Nordidactica*, 2019 (4): 1–27.

Hendek, Abdurrahman. 2021. "Islamic Religious Education in Europe: A Comparative Study", In *Religion & Education*, Vol. 48(4): 499–501.

Hendek, Abdurrahman, and Nigel Fancourt. 2021. "The Effects of Judgements by the European Court of Human Rights on Religious Education in England and Turkey". In *Religion & Education*, Vol 48(4): 436–467.

Hull, John. 1978. "From Christian Nurture to Religious Education: The British Experience." In *Religious Education*, 73: 124–143.

Iversen, Lars. 2012. *Learning to be Norwegian: A Case Study of Identity Management in Religious Education in Norway.* Münster: Waxmann.

Jackson, Robert, and Eleonore Nesbitt. 1993. *Hindu Children in Britain.* Oakhill: Trentham Books.

Jackson, Robert. 1997. *Religious Education: An Interpretive Approach.* London: Hodder and Stoughton.

Jackson, Robert. 2004. *Rethinking Religious Education and Plurality: Issues in Diversity and Pedagogy.* London: Routledge.

Jackson, Robert. 2014. *Signposts – Policy and Practice for Teaching about Religions and Non-Religious World Views in Intercultural Education.* Brussels: Council of Europe Publishing.

Korsvoll, Nils Hallvard. 2021. "A Double Bypass? Tracing How the Aims of Religious Education Are Negotiated across Different Dimensions of the Curriculum in Norway." In *Religion & Education*, Vol. 48(3): 347–363.

Lee, Louis. 2015. *Recognizing the Non-Religious: Reimagining the Secular.* Oxford: Oxford University Press.

Lied, Sissel. 2009. "The Norwegian *Christianity, Religion and Philosophy* subject *KRL* in Strasbourg." In *British Journal of Religious Education*, Vol. 31(3): 263–275.

Lund Johannesen, Øistein, and Geir Skeie. 2018. "Issues in the Integration of Religious Education and Worldviews Education in an Intercultural Context". In *Intercultural Education*, Vol. 30(3): 260–274.

Miedema, Siebren. 2021. "A Postlude on Adequate Methodologies for Comparative Research Regarding the Relation of Religions / Worldview and Education." In *Religion & Education*, Vol. 48(4): 477–489.

Miller, Joyce. 2021. "Reflection on the Seminar on Religion and Education: The Forgotten Dimensions of Religious Education'." In *The Forgotten Dimension of Religious Education?* Edited by Gert Biesta and Patricia Hannam. Leiden / Boston: Brill / Sense, 137–146.

Niemi, Kristian. 2021. "Comparing through Contrasts: Reshaping Incongruence into a Mirror." In *Religion & Education*, Vol. 48(4): 458–476.

Nicolaisen, Tove. 2018. *Hinduer.* Oslo: Universitetsforlaget.

Organization for Security and Co-operation in Europe (OSCE). 2007. *Toledo Guiding Principles on Teaching about Religions and Beliefs in Public Schools: Prepared by ODIHR Advisory Council of Experts on Freedom of Religions and Belief.* Warsaw: OSCE / ODIHR.

Rothgangel, Martin, Robert Jackson, and Martin Jäggle (eds.). 2014. *Religious Education at Schools in Europe. Volume 2: Western Europe.* Göttingen: Vandenhoeck & Ruprecht.

Rothgangel, Martin. 2021a. "Islamic Religious Education in Europe and European Recommendations as Mutual Challenges". In *Islamic Religious Education in Europe: A Comparative Study.* Edited by

Leni Franken and Bill Gent. Routledge Research in Religion and Education, 8. London: Routledge, 249-253.
Rothgangel, Martin. 2021b. "The RE-Puzzle of the Visegrad-Group and the Answer of 'Collective Memory'." In *Religion & Education*, Vol. 48(4): 397-416.
Skeie, Geir. 2013. "A Contextual Turn in Research on Religion and Education?" In *Exploring Context in Religious Education Research. Empirical, Methodological and Theoretical Perspectives.* Edited by Geir Skeie, Judith Everington, Ina ter Avest and Siebren Miedema. Münster: Waxman, 249–272.
Skeie, Geir and, Oddrun Marie Hovde Bråten. 2014. "Religious Education at Schools in Norway" In *Religious Education at Schools in Europe. Volume 3: Northern Europe.* Edited by Martin Rothgangel, Geir Skeie, and Martin Jäggle. Göttingen: Vandenhoeck & Ruprecht, 209-236.
Skeie, Geir. 2017. "Mangfoldets utfordringer og muligheter sett gjennom religionsdidaktisk forskning. Et nordisk overblikk". In *Acta Didactica*, Vol. 11(3): 23.
Weisse, Wolfram. 2010. "REDCo: A European Research Project on Religion and Education". In *Religion & Education*, Vol. 37(3). The Comparative Study of Religion and Education in Europe and Beyond: Contributions of the REDCo Project. https://doi.org/10.1080/15507394.2010.513937
Østberg, Sissel. 1998. *Pakistani Children in Oslo: Islamic Nurture in a Secular Context.* PhD, Coventry, University of Warwick.

Oddrun M. H. Bråten is professor of Religion and Worldviews education, Institute of Education, NTNU. She graduated in Religious Studies at the University of Bergen in 1994 and came to Trondheim in 1998 where she has been working with educating teachers for an inclusive Religious Education school subject since then. This was firstly at the Sør-Trøndelag University College, and since 2016, at the Institute of teacher Education of the Norwegian University of Science and Technology (NTNU). She has a PhD in Education from the University of Warwick (2010) and currently leads NTNU RE Research Group, which is internationally oriented focusing on exploring practice and policy in RE locally, nationally, and internationally. Her work consists of international and comparative studies and empirical research focusing on school and classroom practices. These two research interests are held together by the three-dimensional and four-levels methodology which was developed as part of her PhD, which includes the dimensions of practical teaching in comparative studies. Worldviews education is a newer research interest explored empirically as well as comparatively.

David N. Hempton
From Nonsectarian to Multifaith: An Educational Experiment in Religious Diversity at Harvard ca. 1800–2020

Abstract: The foundation of Harvard University in 1636 and later the Harvard Divinity School (HDS) in 1816 had their roots in puritanical and then nonsectarian Protestantism. By 1816 the original desire to "purify" the faith from Rome had given way to an emphasis on moral unity among Protestant Christians. By then, non-sectarianism implied little more than an attempt to mend fences between Unitarian and Trinitarian Congregationalists. If anything, HDS's liberal Protestant identity was reinforced after the Second World War by President Nathan Pusey who recruited Paul Tillich and pledged to revitalize HDS's Christian mission and ecumenical credentials. Over the next half-century, a complex of changes produced perhaps the most diverse and multireligious divinity school in the United States. How did this happen? In the journey towards a more multireligious school, four innovations are worthy of special treatment: the formation of the Center for the Study of World Religions (1958); the Women's Study in Religion Program (1973); the Pluralism Project (1991); and the creation of the Master in Public Life degree (2020). The purpose of this paper is to identify the social contexts and structural dynamics producing these changes, the theological and philosophical conversations that shaped their expression, and the resistant factors and blind spots that make this story anything but a conventional ascension narrative. Attention will be paid to changing understandings of what constitutes religion and theology, the appropriate categories and social locations for their study, and the engine drivers of change and resistance, which are sometimes more surprising than some metanarratives of increasing religious diversity suggest.

Keywords: Harvard University; multifaith; religious diversity; pluralism.

I am grateful to Amie Montemurro, Jonathan Beasley, Ann Braude, Gordon Hardy, Kristie Welsh, Kathryn Dodgson, William Graham, Shira Telushkin, and Madeline Bugeau-Heartt for their help in researching and writing this essay.

David N. Hempton: John Lord O'Brian Professor of Divinity and Dean of Harvard Divinity School.

The foundations of Harvard University in 1636 and, later, of Harvard Divinity School (HDS) in 1816 had their roots first in puritanical and then nonsectarian Protestantism.[1] By 1816 the original desire to "purify" the faith from Rome had given way to an emphasis on moral unity among Protestant Christians. By then, nonsectarianism implied little more than an attempt to mend fences between Unitarian and Trinitarian Congregationalists. Since then, throughout its history, HDS and the Unitarian Universalist tradition have grown up conjoined. Despite formal nonsectarianism, HDS was founded by Unitarians, nurtured by their support, and shaped from the outset by their interest in non-Christian religions.[2] Interest in other religions, however, did not presuppose equality of esteem. When the transcendentalist James Freeman Clarke examined Asian religions in his course "Ethnic Religions" in the 1870s, he based his reflections on his book *Ten Great Religions* (1871), which argued that non-Christian religions approached truth through the specific cultures of their origins, whereas Christianity was a universal religion divinely adapted to become the religion of all races (Clarke 1871). The cover of the book presents concentric circles, with Judaism and Christianity at the center and other religious traditions and countries of origin distributed around the periphery.

HDS's liberal Protestant and ecumenical identity was reinforced after the Second World War by then Harvard president Nathan Pusey, who recruited Paul Tillich and pledged to revitalize HDS's Christian mission and ecumenical credentials. The Convocation picture of the HDS faculty in 1955, all white men, is a vivid, mid-century testament to the ecumenical aspirations of the School, and to its European philosophical and theological influences. Standing alongside eminent American Unitarian scholars like George Hunston Williams and Conrad Wright are Paul Tillich, Krister Stendahl, the Catholic modernist George LaPiana, the distinguished Jewish philosopher Harry Wolfson, and John A. T. Robinson, later the notorious author of *Honest to God* (1963). Several others had their personal or intellectual roots in Germany, German philosophy and theology, and the German universities.

Over the next half-century, a complex series of changes produced perhaps the most diverse and multireligious divinity school in the United States. How did this happen? Faculty appointments are the easiest to monitor. First, there was a chair

---

[1] For extensive histories of religion at Harvard, see Wiliams 2014 and 1954.

[2] I also want to acknowledge several foundational Harvard Divinity School documents and sources that helped inform this address, including Foundations for a Learned Ministry (Anthony 1992), particularly the opening essay written by the late Reverend Peter J. Gomes; Harvard Divinity Bulletin; the Harvard Divinity School news website, https://hds.harvard.edu/news-events; and the HDS bicentennial exhibit, Faces of Divinity, https://hds.harvard.edu/about/history-and-mission/faces-of-divinity-exhibit. Additionally, for an excellent treatment of Puritanism from a faculty member of Harvard Divinity School, see Hall 2019.

in Roman Catholic theological studies, followed by appointments in Jewish studies, African American religions, Buddhism, Hinduism, Islamic religion and society, comparative theology, and so on. The student body was also changing rapidly with the admission of women and students from non-Protestant Christian backgrounds. In this journey toward a more multireligious school, four innovations, like cardiograph spikes, are worthy of special treatment: the formation of the Center for the Study of World Religions (1958); the Women's Studies in Religion Program (1973); the Pluralism Project (1991); and the creation of the Master of Religion and Public Life degree (2020). The purpose of this essay is to identify the social contexts and structural dynamics producing these changes, the theological and philosophical conversations that shaped their expression, and the resistant factors and blind spots that make this story anything but a conventional ascension narrative. Attention will be paid to changing understandings of what constitutes religion and theology; the appropriate categories and social locations for their study; and the engine drivers of change and resistance, which are sometimes more surprising than some metanarratives of increasing religious diversity suggest.

I would like to start with a personal story, which tends to strike American audiences as strange, though it is more common in other parts of the world, including Europe. I grew up in a working-class Protestant family in East Belfast in the 1950s and '60s and soon entered an educational system that was deeply segregated between Protestants and Catholics. It remains so, even after a quarter of a century since the Good Friday Agreement of 1998 that brought an end to the violent conflict known as the "troubles." Insofar as my memory can be trusted, I have no recollection of ever entering a Catholic school or place of worship before the age of eighteen. The first Catholic place of worship I ever set foot in was as a curious and awestruck tourist to the Cathedral of Santa Maria of Palma on the island of Majorca. To this day, I know that I have visited and attended more worship services in Catholic churches outside of Ireland than within Ireland, despite living most of my life in that country. These educational realities of segregation and denominational exclusivity did not alone cause violence in Ireland, but they have certainly contributed to the separations and stereotypes that often precede and undergird conflict.

My experience of Harvard Divinity School could not be more different. With students from over forty different religious traditions, and a faculty with expertise in many of the world's major religious traditions, HDS is as religiously diverse as any divinity school in the world. How did it get that way? What follows is an attempt to sketch in the broad contours of an unplanned and often unselfconscious educational experiment at Harvard University in creating a multireligious divinity school.

What, then, is a multireligious divinity school? Let's begin with some framing questions. First, there is a terminological problem. There is a paradox in the title itself, because "divinity school" generally connotes Christian, which of course is the religious tradition of HDS's founding and is still its largest tradition as represented by its faculty and students. The phrase "multireligious divinity school" is therefore somewhat problematic, even if alternatives are notoriously hard to come by.

Second, what are the compositional desiderata in a multireligious divinity school? HDS's recent practice has been to appoint professors and enroll students who may be religious practitioners and/or whose primary objective is academic study and scholarship. Some of those professors and students may have no religious beliefs whatsoever and may even be skeptical about religion. That proportion will increase as the share of "nones" and those who are religiously unaffiliated continues to rise as projected in Western societies over the next quarter of a century. Also, in terms of composition: who or what gets to determine the "multi" of multireligious, and how are those decisions made? Explicitly and consciously, based on principles and objectives, or unconsciously and obliquely, based on cultural adaptation and cultural osmosis? The history of HDS seems to suggest that the students, more than professors or administrators, have driven its increasing pluralism. Moreover, what are the appropriate spatial and geographic parameters of "multireligious?" For example, should a divinity school reflect the religious constituencies of its city, its region, its country of location, or the world as a whole? Does Harvard, and do other universities who aspire to global significance and influence, have different criteria for religious diversity than more specifically regional colleges or traditional denominational seminaries?

Third, what are the curricular desiderata of a multireligious divinity school? Specifically, how should religion be studied in a multireligious school? At HDS, and certainly within the historical worlds in which I have operated, there has been a strong emphasis on practice or on what we call "lived religion"—that is, religion with all the messiness of diverse practices, cultural expressions, changes over time, and attention to all of the "religion and . . ." questions. Attention to lived religion in all its forms and expressions means that we also treat current practices seriously, however sharp-edged and exclusive they may be. I do not see it as HDS's job to promote a kind of neutral syncretism. Differences and disagreements need to be honored, not etherized, which leads us to our fourth question.

How does a multireligious divinity school build a community of pluralism, respect, and mutual understanding? How does it construct community rituals, celebrate diverse religious holidays, create welcoming and religiously appropriate gathering spaces, and treat bodies and dress with sensitivity, all without capitulating to some kind of anemic lowest common denominator? Promoting pluralism—not just in theory but in practice—allows each member of our community the opportunity to engage in not just their own religious traditions but the traditions of others. This also allows us to expect and make accommodations, to care as much about the sensitivities of others as about ourselves, and to contribute to community life rather than retreating into sectarian isolation. None of this is automatic or trouble free.

Finally, what does a multireligious divinity school do that a monoreligious school can't (and vice versa)? In a world that is multireligious, an academy that is self-consciously multireligious provides a community context and a curricular content that prepares practitioners and scholars (and combinations of both) for the world into which they will graduate. A multireligious school provides a relatively safe space in which one can experience, study, and work to understand religion in all its complexity and to appreciate difference as a positive reality. In short, this question can be summarized as our "why." Why do we put in the work of ensuring religious diversity for the sake of multifaith education? What benefits will this yield for higher education and for the world at large? The last two points, which I will refer to, in shorthand, as the "how" and the "why," will be where we spend most of our time. In particular: What are the engine drivers and instruments of change? What are the pertinent factors? What are the issues at stake? What are the limiting factors? What are the most pertinent theological issues and scholarly debates?

Let's start with a brief institutional and cultural context. Harvard University was founded by Puritans to advance learning and promote the idea of a learned ministry, an idea rooted in the Puritan sense of vocation, or calling, and the public, civic, and institutional expression of that vocation in both church and state. In recalling the founding acts and metaphors of Harvard College, the public, corporate, civil, *and* religious dimensions cannot be easily separated, and it becomes necessary to relearn the interconnections that, for the Puritan of the seventeenth century, bound up together matters of church and state, private piety and public policy, worldly scholarship, and religious faith. It's not surprising that the first 150 years of Harvard College—from its presidents through its faculty, students, libraries, and pedagogical aspirations—were really directed toward fields that had been a big part of the Puritan tradition. The study of divinity was at the center of a curriculum that was supposed to prepare students for all aspects of life. If you look at those great books of divinity that were written by the seventeenth-century Puritan divines wherever they showed up—especially in the more reformed capitals of Scotland, the Netherlands, and New England—the idea is that all we study reflects the divine character. That's the foundation point. So, you start off from there, then look at the natural world and other aspects of human life. The "professionalization of vocation" as we've come to know it since the eighteenth century, had not yet occurred, and a "profession" was the way one practiced one's vocation. That vocation was to live a godly, righteous, and sober life and to maintain a society in which it was possible to do so. This vocation was both public and comprehensive, and hence the founding of Harvard College was neither an act of the church nor of private patronage and philanthropy but an unambiguous public act of the state in which all aspects of a godly and civilized society were combined. It is, therefore, through the lenses of this concept of vocation that we read the famous passage from *New England's First Fruits*, the earliest account of Harvard College at Cambridge in New England:

> After God had carried us safe to New England and we had built our houses, provided necessaries for our livelihood, reared convenient places for God's worship, and settled the civil government: one of the next things we longed for, and looked after was to advance learning and perpetuate it to posterity; dreading to leave an illiterate ministry to the churches, when our present ministers shall lie in the dust (Eliot 1643).

"Illiterate ministry" refers not simply to those incapable of reading Hebrew, Latin, and Greek, or to those otherwise deprived of the benefits of a university education, but also to those whose sense of vocation was insufficiently capacious for the founding vision of New England. Hence, the nurturing of all society in its godly vocation, not just the church, was to be the central work of Harvard College. A learned ministry was intended for the well-being of all, not simply the elect.

By the 1800s, religion at Harvard had become a hotly disputed affair, and a conscious battle of wills between the Unitarians and the Trinitarians resulted in the emergence of Unitarian dominance in 1805. In 1816, the Society for the Promotion of Theological Education in Harvard University was organized, and its objective was simple: to provide money for instruction in theology and give it to the Harvard Corporation for that purpose. Harvard Divinity School's founding in 1816 was part of the move among Western universities toward the "Enlightenment project," which included an element of separation, an element of specialization, and an element of professionalization. At Harvard, these were represented by the fact that the Divinity School was situated at the edge of campus. This venture was both a serious attempt to improve the training of religious leaders and ministers and a convenient way of allowing Harvard to separate out vocational religious preparation from the wider, more secular University curriculum. By 1826, a curriculum, a faculty, resident graduates, and a building gave ample proof to the existence of Harvard Divinity School. Yet, the School's status was not secure. The problem was not only the perennial one of money, but rather of the political and ecclesiastical conflicts that characterized politics in Massachusetts, from which Harvard was not immune.

In the late 1830s, the School weathered one of its first existential crises. Renowned philosopher and onetime HDS student, Ralph Waldo Emerson, gave a talk, now known as "The Divinity School Address" that "tore them apart," according to historian Stephen Shoemaker (2005). Emerson lambasted the Divinity School for teaching a "corpse cold Unitarianism" that was more interested in promoting ritual and studying the theology of Christ than in living like Christ. While the student body might have been open to such ideas, the faculty was horrified, and Emerson was shunned for thirty years. Controversies surrounding Emerson's views and their social and cultural ramifications were not the only controversies embroiling the Divinity School. Its first dean, John Gorham Palfrey, was an abolitionist who was expressly forbidden by two successive Harvard presidents and its governing corporation from propagating antislavery views on campus. He was effectively forced out and eventually given a government commission by Abraham Lincoln. More durably, the well-known status shifts of the nineteenth century away from theology and toward the natural sciences persuaded growing numbers of Harvard faculty that a modern, evolving institution of higher education should not deal at all in the partisan and irrational speculations of theology.

But, during the years 1877–1879, Harvard president Charles William Eliot made a compelling case for the existence of a nondenominational, nonsectarian, graduate divinity school, arguing that Harvard and the country needed such a place:

> Let at least one University school of theology be suitably supported, where young men may study theology and the kindred subjects with the same freedom of spirit with which they study law in law school or medicine in medical school, and with as little intention or opportunity of committing themselves prematurely to any particular set of opinions or practices (James 1930, 368).

President Eliot concluded his forty-year tenure in 1909 with an address at the Divinity School, "The Religion of the Future," in which he saw, somewhat optimistically, less doctrine, less denominationalism, and more moral and spiritual consensus along the lines of the scientific religious inquiry and cooperation he had championed at Harvard (Eliot 1909). Some of Eliot's successors were not so enthusiastic about the role of religion in a serious university. James Bryant Conant, who served as Harvard president from 1933 to 1953, had a noted distaste for religion, and he deliberately permitted the Divinity School to wither on the vine. But in 1953, the newly appointed president, Nathan Marsh Pusey, revitalized the Divinity School. In his 1953 Divinity School Convocation Address, Pusey stated: "It is leadership in religious knowledge, and even more, in religious experience—not increased industrial might, not more research facilities, certainly not these things by themselves—of which we now have a gaping need." Not many university presidents of elite universities in the West could make such a statement now.

How then can we explain the growing religious diversity of HDS since the Second World War? One example of how the School adapted to the social context of the 1960s was by developing a new degree program for a new era. In 1968, the introduction of the Master of Theological Studies (MTS) degree and a new doctoral field in comparative religion expanded the School's recruitment beyond

Protestants and Unitarian Universalist candidates, most of them men, pursuing the professional degree in ministry. The 1970s and 1980s saw a dramatic and permanent shift in the student population: women became at least half of each entering class. Gradually, students from other religious groups joined Protestant ministry candidates. Students enrolled in the MTS for predoctoral work, as well to combine training in religion with other professional fields. With the adoption of a new curriculum in 1981, MTS students could concentrate in non-Christian religions, as well as study Christianity. Faculty appointments outside of Christian studies attracted an increasingly diverse student population. While most faculty saw this as an expansion of the School's historic commitments, a few regretted the decentering of Christianity. No formal decision determined that HDS would become a multireligious school. Change came incrementally by curricular decision.

This period also included major shifts in leadership. One of the most influential Europeans at HDS was Swedish theologian and New Testament scholar Krister Stendahl, who served as dean from 1968 to 1979. The early years of his administration were marked by the social and academic turbulence characteristic of higher education institutions in this period. The war in Vietnam was debated passionately within the Divinity School community, and such symbolic gestures as offering of sanctuary in Andover Chapel to a draft resister and the flying of the red flag from Andover Hall served to remind the Divinity School that it was not isolated from current affairs. Throughout this time—one of the most tumultuous political eras of American history, on college campuses and elsewhere—Stendahl successfully guided HDS with an astute, sometimes blunt, decisiveness that was tempered by his wry humor and his enormous gift for listening. Stendahl served as Bishop of Stockholm, Sweden, from 1984 to 1988, but returned to HDS in the late 1980s to become the School's first chaplain, a much more important undertaking than the title at first suggested, given the ethos of religious pluralism, and related pedagogical approach, that had developed further at HDS in the 1980s. At the time, Stendahl explained his vision for his new assignment in this way:

> In our community there is no one form, name, or liturgy which can claim the allegiance of all. To be a chaplain in this place therefore must mean to help worship happen in many forms at many times and to guard fiercely the freedom of every person to pray and speak in ways important to him or her—lest the specter of "pluralism" mute authentic expression of devotion (Joyner 2008).

Any attempt to explain the increasing religious diversity of Harvard Divinity School and the wider University in this period must reckon with the impact of the Center for the Study of World Religions (CSWR), founded in the late 1950s. The controversies surrounding its formation tell you a great deal about the intellectual currents of this period regarding the place of religion in the curriculum of an aspiring world-class university (Carman and Dogson 2006, 11–14). The all-important donors for this new venture were mostly Anglicans influenced by the Theosophical Movement. Their leader, known anonymously as "the lady," was partly inspired by the existence of the Spalding Professorship of Eastern Religion and Ethics at Oxford University, the first holder of which was Sarvepalli Radhakrishnan, who later became president of India. Neither HDS nor the wider Harvard University was united behind the idea of establishing the CSWR, or even where it should be located. Superimposed on the inevitable turf wars over power and influence, in which universities specialize, were complex intellectual and ideological disagreements over whether religion should be taught as phenomenology in the Faculty of Arts and Sciences or as lived practices at the Divinity School, or, as some would have it, not at all. In the end, money talked. As Krister Stendahl later explained it, the donors expressed a strong preference for the Divinity School being the home base for the Center because "they feared that unless it was related to a theological faculty, the tendency would win out by which the emphasis on language studies, etc., would short-change the emphasis on contemporary manifestations of the faith" (Carman and Dogson 2006, 13–14). Even so, the faculty of the Divinity School were not themselves united on the wisdom of having the CSWR attached to their school. Those influenced by German Protestant theology wanted HDS to concentrate solely on educating Protestant ministers and were concerned about the possible long-term decentering of Christianity. As time has shown, neither of these concerns proved groundless. Only a small minority of students currently enrolled at HDS are bound for ministry in a Protestant tradition.

In the foundation of the CSWR, accepting the money and establishing the location was far from the end of the matter. The new center needed a professor and director, which occasioned even more complicated ideological and practical disagreements. The desired appointee, it was decided, should have both scholarly credentials and administrative and political skills. Moreover, the ideal appointee should have familiarity with at least one major Asian or "world" religion. But there was also distrust of appointing someone from a missionary background, which would not sit well with the postcolonial critique of Western proselytism and imperialism. On the other hand, there was a desire not to appoint someone solely within a historicist, objective approach to the study of religion that was deemed heavy on post-Enlightenment disciplinary scholarship and light on theology. Who would now want to be on this search committee?

As it turned out, it did not matter. After failing to lure the Islamic scholar Wilfred Cantwell Smith from McGill University, HDS dean Douglas Horton offered the position to Robert H. L. Slater, Cambridge University–educated and formerly an Anglican chaplain at the University of Rangoon in Burma, who had done his doctoral work on Theravada Buddhism at Columbia University and published books drawing on his wartime experiences in Burma and on his expertise in both Christianity and Buddhism. As John Carman, a future director of the CSWR, put it, "in addition to the difficult ideological objections to the new chair in world religions from secular philosophers, traditional historians, and neo-orthodox Protestant theologians, the first holder of the chair had to begin with his faculty colleagues resentful of the high-handed action of their dean," who had already disturbed the theological waters with his recent approval of a new chair in Roman Catholic studies (Carman and Dogson 2006, 17).

Slater was charged with a formidable list of tasks: to encourage the study of the great religions of the world; to create a world religions graduate program; to encourage a sympathetic understanding of religions; to encourage spiritual conversations between people of different religious faiths; and to facilitate the creation of works of art, music, or literature that would stimulate the sympathetic understanding of the religions of the world. Despite the challenges confronting him, Slater did a remarkable job of achieving many of these objectives and also succeeded in opening the Josep Lluís Sert–designed CSWR building in 1960, recruiting distinguished faculty like Robert Bellah and Masatoshi Nagatomi, and overseeing a peaceful transfer of power to his successor as director, Wilfred Cantwell Smith. The Center was sent on its way, with a stirring speech at the opening of the Sert building by the then vice-president of India, Sarvepalli Radhakrishnan:

> In every religion we have people who do not believe in provincialism, who emphasise religion as experience to be attained by self-conquest and self-transformation, appreciation of other faiths, and a sense of loyalty to the world community. If man is to achieve wholeness for himself and for the world, if he seeks harmonious living, he must know other religions. We must set aside differences caused by the accidents of geography and history and accept the universal ideas transmitted by a common heritage [...].
> The different religions should be regarded as comrades in a joint enterprise in facing the common problems of the peaceful coexistence of the peoples, international welfare and justice, racial equality and political independence of all peoples (Radhakrishnan 1961, 39).

Perhaps the clearest testimony of the achievement of the early objectives of the CSWR comes from the pen of William Graham, the distinguished Islamicist and former dean of HDS, who joined one of the earliest cohorts of doctoral students associated with the CSWR. He came to the CSWR in 1966, two years into Cantwell Smith's directorship. He writes warmly of Smith's relentless attempts to create "a multi-traditional and multi-linguistic intellectual community of scholars" dedicated to the comparative study of religion through the widest possible geographical and conceptual lenses. According to Graham, Smith thought that

> the CSWR was [...] the one place in North America, maybe even the world, where such study and reflection was assumed to be the baseline for conversation, corporate and individual

investigation, and cutting-edge intellectual exploration. Furthermore, he was convinced that the Christocentric curricula, not only at Christian seminaries, but also at university divinity schools such as Harvard's, were inadequate to the serious investigation of religion as a pan-human, global phenomenon of critical importance to culture and history everywhere (Graham 2006, 4–5).

The chief challenges to these expansive aspirations were the Christocentricity of the Divinity School and the unwillingness of the rest of Harvard to take religion seriously. But there were also self-imposed ideological limitations. For example, before the 1970s, the indigenous religions of Africa were excluded from the CSWR because of the view that they lacked written scriptures. Visiting African students, some of whom were political exiles, saw this as yet another expression of Western colonialism. A tour of African universities in 1974 by John Carman, a scholar of Hinduism and comparative religion and director of the CSWR at the time, and the eminent African American scholar, Preston Williams, helped turn the tide at the CSWR and HDS, resulting in several important appointments in African religious traditions.

Over the six decades of its existence, the Center has worked to create a multi-religious space, in which interfaith understanding was developed both in academic work and in shared meals, late-night conversations, and the cultivation of a common garden. Among the many distinguished visiting faculty members who have been a part of life at the CSWR, the Spanish priest and comparative philosopher Raimon Panikkar was one of the most influential. In residence at the CSWR between 1967 and 1971, he mirrored the Center's comparative perspective. Reflecting later on his time of pilgrimage in India, he wrote: "I 'left' [Europe] as a christian, I 'found' myself a hindu, and I 'return' a buddhist, without having ceased to be a christian" (Panikkar 199, 42). In 1979, the fourteenth Dalai Lama made his first trip to the United States. His final stop, at the invitation of the CSWR, was Harvard, where he gave a lecture and taught a seminar to HDS students. He has come back repeatedly—in 1981, 1995, 2003, and 2009.

How then are we to evaluate the achievements and limitations of the CSWR in light of its ambitious original objectives? This is a hard question to answer. Any evaluation of the CSWR under its seven directors—many of them, ironically, with missionary backgrounds—must consider the different priorities of its leaders and scholars, which serve almost as a chronological and intellectual barometer of the prevailing currents and fashions in the study of religion.[3] But there are three

---

3   The first three directors developed fields of study in Buddhism, Islam, and Hinduism; the fourth focused on South American and Indigenous religious traditions without written scriptures. More

inescapable conclusions. The first is that the CSWR has inexorably reshaped the curriculum of the Divinity School in the direction of a world religions focus and helped make it one of the most religiously diverse divinity schools in the world. The second is that the CSWR became a temporary home for hundreds of distinguished scholars of world religions who then carried their newly refined expertise to all parts of the world. Third, the various controversies that surrounded the creation of the CSWR have never gone away. The role of religion in the various schools and curricula of wider Harvard is still contested territory. The old Enlightenment-inspired hostility to the teaching of religion in a great research university and its multiple graduate schools has persisted, despite what many readers of this essay might regard as the inescapable importance of developing religious literacy in a world in sore need of it.

Whether or not religion ought to be taught in a research university is one thing; how it is to be taught is another. In facing that issue, none of the following questions will be news to readers. What is the relationship between insider and outside perspectives? How can, or should, conservative and fundamentalist perspectives be incorporated into curricula and reflected in faculty appointments and student enrollments? Has the old comparative approach to the study of religion run out of steam, along with its sometimes-naïve sister, ecumenical dialogue? What counts as religion, and who sets the agenda for its study? As we judge the intellectual blinkers and limitations of past scholars on how to think about the category of religion, what are ours, and how would we recognize them?

Another milestone of comparable importance to the founding of the CSWR in the growing diversity of HDS's approach to the study of religion was the formation of the Women's Studies in Religion Program. Women were admitted to HDS in 1955 as part of the expansion of the School's mission to train leaders for the international ecumenical movement. By 1969, a total of twenty-three women had graduated, and never more than three in a single year. In a dramatic reversal, women would compose a majority of students by 1980 and would remain at least half of each class from then on. If women were to become religious leaders, millennia of scholarship supporting their exclusion had to be critiqued, reformed, or contradicted. Women's studies started as an approach to women's ministry but expanded to ask what difference gender makes in every field taught at HDS. Increasing enrollment of women students coincided with the blossoming of feminism in the 1970s. In a 1971 HDS course, women in the class blew noisemakers and kazoos whenever a masculine pronoun was used to refer to human beings or, more controversially, to God.

---

recent directors have focused on environmental sustainability and on transcendence and transformation in spiritual traditions.

After classmate E. J. Dionne reported on the class in the student newspaper, *The Harvard Crimson*, members of the Department of Linguistics ridiculed the action as "pronoun envy." Then *Newsweek* magazine picked up the story. In 2014, *The New Yorker* published HDS alumna Anne Carson's poem about the incident. The result is that this has become a famous early assertion of inclusive language and represents the impact HDS students have as agents for change.

The Women's Studies in Religion Program (WSRP) was founded in 1973 in response to the need to transform theological education to reflect the unprecedented presence of women as candidates for the ministry and students of religion. The WSRP was established not only as a place of diversifying representation but as a bedrock for a newly institutionalizing area of study: that of women and religion. Constance Buchanan, a faculty member and associate dean at HDS for twenty years, is credited with leading the WSRP to become an internationally recognized center for research on faith, gender, race, and sexual orientation. Buchanan became director of the WSRP in 1977, and she had the foresight to reach outside academia to find philanthropic women with passions and interests that intersected with the WSRP's mission, even though many of them had no direct Harvard connections. Among the frustrations of building a "new" and lasting body of scholarship centering on women's stories is the fact that many of the women predecessors working decades, even centuries, prior to the founding of the WSRP have consistently been ignored, forgotten, or erased. As our current WSRP director, Ann Braude, said:

> Men have thousands of years of religious scholarship, performed exclusively by men for men from a male point of view. Men were the only ones who had access to education and access to the languages, access to the technical and intellectual and scholastic skills. There were always women with stories. There were always women intellectuals. There were always women asking questions. But there wasn't an institutionalized way to build.[4]

The WSRP sought to remedy that deficiency by bringing five research associates every year to teach students, give a public lecture, and complete a major research project. Over 200 women have benefited from this program, and many have gone on to influential academic or professional appointments in the United States and all around the world.

A third important milestone in HDS's and wider Harvard's multireligious journey was the creation of the Pluralism Project. In 1991, HDS Professor Diana Eck, who had been deeply involved with the CSWR as a student, first offered the Harvard course "World Religions in New England." The subject matter came organically from her growing interest in the shifting religious landscape of the United States, a

---

4   Ann Braude, interview by HDS student Madeline Bugeau-Heartt, March 2022.

trend that could be seen in the changing face of the student body at Harvard. Twenty-five students joined Eck in the inaugural course, and together they set out to explore the increasingly diverse religious communities in the Boston area:

> When I first met these new students—Muslims from Providence, Hindus from Baltimore, Sikhs from Chicago, Jains from New Jersey—they signaled to me the emergence in America of a new cultural and religious reality about which I knew next to nothing. At that point I had not been to an American mosque, I had never visited a Sikh community in my own country, and I could imagine a Hindu summer camp only by analogy with my Methodist camp experience. I felt the very ground under my feet as a teacher and scholar begin to shift. My researcher's eye began to refocus—from Banaras to Detroit, from Delhi to Boston (Eck 2001, 17–18).

From the Sri Lakshmi Temple to New England's first mosque, students documented the post–Immigration Act (1965) transformation of Greater Boston's religious makeup. The result of this research was the publishing of *World Religions in Boston: A Guide to Communities and Resources*, a printed guidebook that would serve as a model for future research. The Pluralism Project engaged the best energies of Harvard students from both the Faculty of Arts and Sciences and the Divinity School (the oft-sought-after cross-university collaboration) in "hometown" research and in such cities as Denver, Houston, and Minneapolis. Some had a more specific focus: Hindu summer camps in Pennsylvania, Vietnamese Buddhist struggles with zoning laws in California, the annual convention of the Islamic Society of North America in Kansas City, or the history of the Interfaith Conference of Metropolitan Washington, D.C. Each year, during the subsequent fall semester, the researchers presented their work at a Pluralism Project research conference. Over the course of its existence the Pluralism Project has experimented with film and case method teaching and focused attention on immigration, teachers and school curricula, and women's religious networks. In 1998, President Bill Clinton recognized Eck with the national humanities award, explicitly for the contribution of the Pluralism Project to national culture.

Discussing the Pluralism Project and its exceptional online content is an excellent transition to the expanded digital age we have experienced in the last two decades. As more information became available through the Internet and geographical distance became less of a barrier, thanks to online engagement, the digital age brought to light many opportunities—and many challenges from our past. As for opportunities, HDS has seen a boom in online engagement. Faculty members have created Massive Open Online Courses (MOOCs) that are offered for free to those who audit. HDS is now in its sixth year of offering such courses, including one titled "World Religions Through Their Scriptures," which have together registered around one million participants from over 150 countries. HDS has also benefited from expanding events with digital access and sharing lessons learned from visiting scholars and monastics with wider audiences.

So, we have made our way to the current decade and the endpoint mentioned in my title, 2020, when HDS launched a new program called Religion and Public Life (RPL). We talk about this program as a canopy, which covers many different elements, such as Religious Literacy in the Professions and the Religion, Conflict, and Peace Initiative, to engage professionals in a range of fields traditionally thought of as secular. They join the HDS community for a year or two, connect with our students, staff, and faculty, work on a research project or book, and create networks to further expand what has become the mission of this program—creating a just world at peace. We also developed a new master's program to bolster this work, the master of religion and public life degree, which is the first new degree program at the School since we launched the master of theological studies in the 1960s.

In the past several years, we have seen trends, both from our own admissions numbers and from large organizations such as Pew Research Center, that show people's engagement with religion is shifting. Simultaneously, we have seen an increased number of students who identify as "no affiliation" or "spiritual but not religious," along with students reconnecting with faith traditions that have been marginalized from academia and students from any number of traditions who are concerned less with their own doctrine and more with learning how to connect across differences. For these reasons, among many others, we felt the urgent need to build out an academic home, if you will, for anyone interested in exploring religion through the lens of public life—activism, education, government, humanitarian action, journalism, law, media, medicine, public policy, and so on. This program filled a long-felt need to create space for those interested in the study of religion who are not interested in ministry studies or traditional theological scholarship. In many ways, this program has brought us back to our roots: that ideal of a learned ministry informing the evolving concept of vocation—the notion that piety, policy, and the public weal were all expressions of the divine will.

Going back to some of the challenges mentioned earlier: Increased access to information and expanded audiences has also brought issues related to representation, equity, and justice into clearer focus for many of us—a reckoning, if you will. Whose voices have been centered, and whose voices have been subjugated? What perspectives have dominated the narrative, and what perspectives have been underrepresented? This work includes learning more about Harvard University's involvement in removing native peoples from their land and its complicity in slavery. A sobering recent report released by the University, *Harvard and the Legacy of*

Slavery, tells uncomfortable and hard truths, one of which is that HDS itself was partly funded by money made out of the slave trade and the slave economy.[5]

What this report has made clear is that it is not enough simply to recognize subjugation and injustice. Rather, a genuine look at our past must also involve meaningful action to do better now and build a just future for all. Under the leadership of our School's associate dean for diversity, inclusion, and belonging, our aim is to actively build an antiracist and anti-oppressive Harvard Divinity School—which means that our students, staff, faculty, alumni, and supporters, and those who engage with the HDS community, are learning valuable lessons about how to address bias, promote equality, and understand intersectionality. That also involves grappling with the difficult dichotomy shared by many institutions within higher education that simultaneously represent truth and knowledge while steeped in histories entangled with oppression and injustice.

As my title suggests, HDS is still an educational experiment, and only time will tell where the future of religious diversity in education will take us. The first step is to better understand and reckon with our past. The two most important questions to answer are: What were the engines driving the transition from nonsectarian to multireligious at HDS? And what were its chief characteristics and limitations? The answer to the first question must pay attention to the profound cultural shifts in the post–Second World War era, including deep unease over colonialism and the impact of decolonization, the rise of feminism and women's participation in higher education, the influence of multiculturalism and pluralism, the growth of international travel and experiences of globalism, and the widening of educational opportunities to different social groups and constituencies through technology. HDS had the advantage, perceived so only in retrospect, of having weak ties to any formal religious tradition or establishment and hence few financial, theological, or intellectual obligations to religious institutions or controlling authorities beyond Harvard itself. The School, to my knowledge, never set out with a clear ideological agenda or institutional plan to become a multifaith institution. As much driven by student demand as by institutional strategy, by cultural shifts as by considered priorities, and by donor desiderata as by academic rationale, the "multireligious move" was episodic, pragmatic, and contested. The trajectory was nevertheless fairly consistently in an increasingly diverse direction, with cardiograph-like spikes around the formation of the Center for the Study of World Religions, the Women's Studies in Religion Program, the Pluralism Project, and Religion and Public Life. Moreover, there are clearly parallels between the story of increasing religious

---

5 *The Legacy of Slavery at Harvard: Report and Recommendations of the Presidential Committee* (Cambridge, MA: Harvard University Press, 2022).

pluralism at HDS and in the roughly coterminous history of the United States. HDS is probably the most religiously plural divinity school in the United States, and the United States, depending on chosen criteria, is one of the most religiously plural countries in the world.[6] Claims to American exceptionalism are generally worth resisting, but it is hard to imagine that HDS could have developed the way it has in states with a closer connection between religious establishments and political power.

The second question, about the characteristics and limitations of HDS's multireligious experiment, is easier to figure out, even if it is not always straightforward. HDS grew out of settler colonialism, religious independence, and a progressive bent that has always been part of its tradition. There are some obvious ironies. HDS has always been better at critiquing other people's empires than in paying attention to the religious traditions of native or enslaved peoples, or even the religious consequences of America's own imperial entanglements in places like the Korean peninsula. There is still no established chair at HDS on the religions of Indigenous people, and only recently could one say that Africana diasporic and African American religious traditions have been treated with the seriousness they deserve. Similarly, only lately have we paid attention to the very close connections between American and Korean evangelicalism in the Cold War era through parachurch organizations like the Billy Graham Evangelistic Association, Campus Crusade for Christ, and World Vision (Kim 2022). American evangelicalism has taken on more of a nationalistic hue over the past several decades, but that should not draw attention away from its less well-studied trans-Atlantic and trans-Pacific influences (e.g. Stanley 2013).

What one can say with certitude from this brief survey of an important educational experiment is that the categories for studying religion have steadily expanded over the past two centuries, and that trend is not going to stop. Neither will the university turf wars between those who regard the study of religion as an unfortunate vestigial remnant in the modern academy and those who see religion as a primary characteristic of the human condition, past, present, and future, that needs to be treated with both analytical sophistication and a degree of critical empathy. If current trends continue, HDS will be enrolling more and more students who self-identify as religiously unaffiliated or as spiritual but not religious and who have growing interests in religious traditions beyond the conventional world

---

6 According to the global religious diversity index constructed by the Pew Research Center, the United States, because of its high proportion of Christians, counts as only moderately diverse, even though the sheer number of different religious traditions represented in its population is quite high.

religions paradigm. As the climate crisis becomes more urgent, there will be a special interest in religious traditions, ancient and modern, that have something to offer a burning and flooding planet. As ever, students and the wider culture will help determine the shape of change, and educational institutions and their faculties will have to adapt or disappear. Many denominational seminaries in Greater Boston and throughout the United States have already closed. The content of religious and theological education is also changing rapidly. At HDS, during its two centuries-long journey from a nonsectarian to a multifaith institution, what counts as multifaith has changed from encountering other traditions in order to missionize them more effectively, to learning *about* them out of academic curiosity, to learning *from* them out of epistemic humility, and, inexorably, to learning *with* them as collaborative partners.

References

Anthony, Michael J. 1992. *Foundations for a Learned Ministry*. Cambridge, MA: Harvard Divinity School.

Carman, John B. and Kathryn Dodgson. 2006. *Community and Colloquy: The Center for the Study of World Religions, 1958–2003*. Cambridge, MA: Center for the Study of World Religions, Harvard Divinity School.

Clarke, James Freeman. 1871. Ten Great Religions: An Essay in Comparative Theology. Boston: s.n.

Eck, Diana L. 2001. A New Religious America: How a "Christian Country" Has Become the World's Most Religiously Diverse Nation. New York: HarperCollins.

Eliot, Charles W. 1909. *The Religion of the Future*. Boston: J. W. Luce.

Eliot, John. 1643. *New England's First Fruits*. London.

Graham, William A. 2006. "Foreword". In Carman, John B. and Kathryn Dodgson. 2006. *Community and Colloquy: The Center for the Study of World Religions, 1958–2003*. Cambridge, MA: Center for the Study of World Religions, Harvard Divinity School.

Hall, David D. 2019. *The Puritans: A Transatlantic History*. Princeton, NJ: Princeton University Press.

James, Henry. *Charles W. Eliot*. Vol. 1. Boston: Houghton Mifflin.

Joyner, Will. 2008. "Krister Stendahl, 1921–2008." In *Harvard Divinity School News Archive*, 16 April 2008. https://newsarchive.hds.harvard.edu/news/2011/02/07/krister-stendahl-1921-2008.

Kim, Helen Jin. 2022. Race for Revival: How Cold War South Korea Shaped the American Evangelical Empire. New York: Oxford University Press.

Panikkar, Raimon. 1999. *The Intra-Religious Dialogue*. New York: Paulist Press.

Radhakrishnan, Sarvepalli. 1961. *Fellowship of the Spirit*. Cambridge, MA: Center for the Study of World Religions; Harvard University Press.

Shoemaker, Stephen P. 2005. Dyspeptics, Mystics, and Skeptics: The Evolution of a Scholarly Approach to Religion at Nineteenth Century Harvard. PhD diss., Harvard University.

Stanley, Brian. 2013. *The Global Diffusion of Evangelicalism*. Downers Grove, IL: InterVarsity Press.

Williams, George Huntston. 2014. *Divinings: Religion at Harvard from Its Origins in New England Ecclesiastical History to the 175th Anniversary of the Harvard Divinity School, 1636–1992*, edited by Rodney L. Petersen, 3 vols. Göttingen: Vandenhoeck & Ruprecht.

Williams, George Huntston. 1954. *The Harvard Divinity School: Its Place in Harvard University and in American Culture*. Boston: Beacon Press.

David N. Hempton is John Lord O'Brian Professor of Divinity and Dean of Harvard Divinity School. He held prior appointments as Director of the School of History at Queen's University Belfast and distinguished University Professor at Boston University. He is a Fellow of the Royal Historical Society and an Honorary Member of the Royal Irish Academy. He has delivered the Cadbury Lectures at the University of Birmingham, the F. D. Maurice Lectures at King's College, London, and the Gifford Lectures at the University of Edinburgh. His books include *Methodism and Politics in British Society 1750-1850* (Stanford University Press, 1984), winner of the Whitfield Prize of the Royal Historical Society; *Methodism: Empire of the Spirit* (Yale University Press, 2005), *Evangelical Disenchantment: Nine Portraits of Faith and Doubt* (Yale University Press, 2008), *The Church in the Long Eighteenth Century* (I. B. Tauris, 2011), winner of the Albert C. Outler Prize of the American Society of Church History; and most recently (with Hugh McLeod), *Secularization and Religious Innovation in the North Atlantic World* (Oxford University Press, 2017). He is currently preparing a book from the 2021 Gifford Lectures.

Halina Grzymała-Moszczyńska
The Role of Religion in Coping with Refugee Trauma: Agency and Resilience

Abstract: Research and general discourse represent refugees in terms of helplessness and loss. This representation consigns their bodies to a mute and faceless physical mass. This paper attempts to build a more detailed picture of who they are and present the role of religion in the agency and resilience of forced migrants coping with refugee trauma.

Three different approaches to the mental health of refugees will be discussed. The first two are concerned with disorder etiology, and the third is concerned with getting well. The oldest of the three is the War Displacement Model, which directly connects disorders in migrants' functioning with experienced wartime trauma, violence and loss. A second approach, the Ecological Displacement-Related Model, emerged from research concentrated on both the conditions of military conflict victims living in their country during the conflict and after they have escaped. The third approach is the ADAPT model (Adaptation and Development After Trauma and Persecution): it focuses on the conditions that individuals, who have experienced warfare and persecution related trauma, must meet to get healthy again.

Results from my field research conducted during 25 years among various groups of refugees including Bosnians, Kosovars, Armenians from Upper Karabach, Chechens and Syrians will provide examples of the role of religion in supporting agency and resilience amidst different hardships inherent in refugees' situation.

Keywords: psychology of religion, refugees, resilience, agency

1 Introduction

My entire academic career has been connected—and still is—with the Psychology of Religion. This borderline discipline belongs to Psychology and Religious Studies

---

Halina Grzymała-Moszczyńska is Professor of Psychology at the Ignatianum University of Krakow, Poland.

but gets involved with Cultural Psychology at times. That border is not easy to cross, as it will appear from two real stories I will tell you.

I call the first one "The Knife".

In the late Nineties, I was about to leave for my research trip among refugees from Kosovo. When I was almost on the threshold of the University building, a colleague stopped me and asked: "By the way, Halina, do you have a knife?". That was kind of a shock. "A knife? For what?" "You know... You are going to do research... You are going to meet the Kosovar refugees... They are Muslims, and they might be dangerous: they might rape you".

The other story reports events that occurred some years later during my research among the Upper Karabakh people.

They were Armenian Christians who came to Poland because of the war in Upper Karabakh; they went to the local Roman-Catholic church to see a local priest and ask for a memorial service for their compatriots who perished in the war. The priest met them with this simple statement: "Go to your sheikh". He couldn't believe that people from Armenia could be anything but Muslims, so the sheikh had to be the best option.

Speaking more in detail about the refugee groups I investigated over the years, they consisted of subgroups I researched in Poland (Bosnian, Kosovar, Upper Karabakh, Chechens, and Afghan refugees) and abroad (Syrian refugees in Turkey and Jordan).

I also participated in the research among refugee groups of *Scholars at Risk* (scholars who fled to Western countries because of persecution suffered at their home universities) and artists hosted by the ICORN Network (International Cities of Refuge Network, a protection network aiming at supporting persecuted artists).

Religious identities of researched groups were very diverse: Muslims, Christians (both Assyrian and Armenian) and atheists.

Multiple research groups, as well as multiple sites of research, taught me a lesson, which could be summarised as follows: do not essentialise refugees, and be careful with general labels attributed to refugees irrespectively of their other characteristics such as age, gender, country of destination and social capital they can bring with them. Such a critical reflection gets applied when building the analytical network to investigate the role of religion in coping with refugee trauma.

2 The Concept of Refugee Trauma

In the 1980 definition by the American Psychiatric Association, two aspects of an event implicate trauma: unusual character and the strength of the stressor.

> The stressor producing this syndrome would evoke significant symptoms of distress in most people and is generally outside such common experiences as bereavement, chronic illness, business losses, or martial conflict. The trauma may be experienced alone (rape or assault) or in the company of groups of people (military combat). Stressors producing this disorder include natural disasters (floods, earthquakes), accidental man-made disasters (car accidents with serious physical injury, airplane crushes, large fires), or deliberate man-made disasters (bombing, torture, death camps) (American Psychiatric Association 1980, 236).

However, over time this definition has undergone some changes. In the fourth edition of the *Diagnostic and Statistical Manual of Mental Disorders*, the definition of trauma included a response to a life- or health-threatening or physical integrity-threatening event that a person experienced, witnessed, or had to confront:

> exposure to an extreme traumatic stressor involving direct personal experience of an event that involves actual or threatened death or serious injury, or other threat to one's physical integrity; or witnessing an event that involves death, injury, or a threat to the physical integrity of another person; or learning about unexpected or violent death, serious harm, or threat of death or injury experienced by a family member or other close associate (American Psychiatric Association 2000, 463).

Thus, for the first time, the component of subjective perception of an event was included, which implies that not every person experiencing the same event will perceive it as traumatic.

The fifth edition of the *Diagnostic and Statistical Manual of Mental Disorders* underlines secondary trauma also caused by learning that such an event

> occurred to a close family member or close friend (in case of actual or threatened death of a family member or friend, the event(s) must have been violent or accidental); or experiencing repeated or extreme exposure to aversive details of the traumatic event(s) (American Psychiatric Association 2022, 301).

3 Building the Analytical Framework

Why do we need a deconstruction strategy while analysing religion's role in coping with refugee trauma? The brief answer is that we need it because of the competing perspectives on the role of religion.

Religion is conceived simultaneously as a positive factor contributing to survival under traumatic conditions, a negative factor causing refugee trauma, and a factor contributing to recovery after refugee trauma.

Deconstructing competing perspectives and theoretical concepts is necessary to enhance further understanding of the problem.

The deconstruction of the concepts is in the service of diversity: we need to specify sub-categories of refugees (their location, age, background, gender, and family situation); we need to detail different periods in their refugeehood; and finally, we also have to be careful about which methodological paradigms and research methods are employed by researchers who approach refugees, and offer their findings after analysis of collected research material.

Conducting such deconstruction will give justice to the diversity of subgroups in the refugee population and contribute further to the theoretical, analytical framework of analysis.

Two theoretical concepts are particularly relevant here. They are resilience and agency.

Resilience, as defined by the Dictionary of the American Psychological Association (VandenBos 2007), is the successful adaptation through flexibility to complex or challenging life experiences creating mental, emotional, and behavioural demands. There are several factors contributing to resilience: just to name a few, how individuals view and engage with the world, the availability and quality of social resources, and the specific coping strategies employed by the individuals. In the case of refugee groups, one more contributing factor is the specificity of the reaction of a particular receiving country *vis à vis* refugees.

Agency is the capability to influence one's functioning and the course of events through one's actions (Bandura 1989). The pillars of agency are the following: intentionality—action plans and strategies; anticipation—ability and process to envisage an outcome of the action and act accordingly toward it; self-reactivity—self-regulatory processes that integrate thought and action; and self-reflection—ability to reflect upon own behaviours, awareness of motives and inspirations bringing desired outcomes. The individual intends to influence the situation in a certain way because of the specific output, intention, reflection, expectation of results of the one's action, and a reflection of what might happen as the result of an undertaken activity.

The concepts of agency and resilience are intertwined. Figure 1 demonstrates the intricate structure of this mutual relationship.

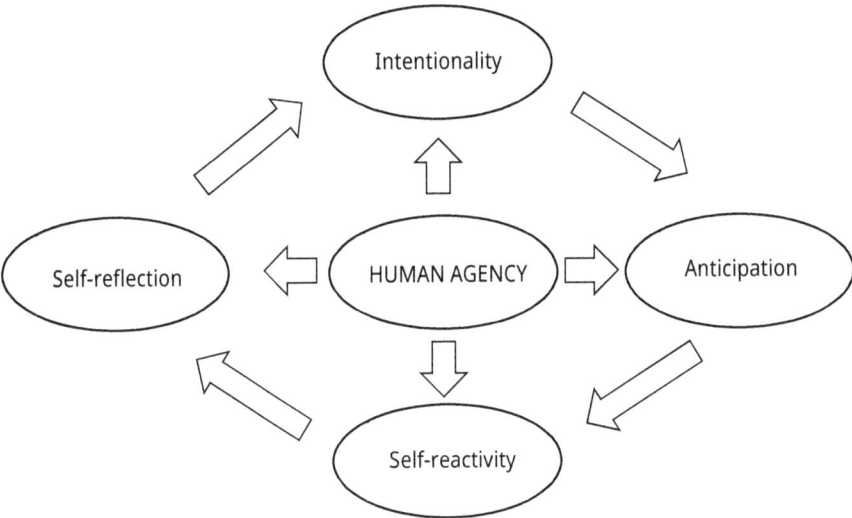

Fig. 1: Psychological Agency (Lima, Nassif and Garçon 2020)

Resilience after refugee trauma is a precondition for restoring agency. Agency will not be present if people do not end the process with adaptation. Therefore, agency demonstrates restored resilience and aims at getting control of and activity in the situation.

4 Defining Refugees

Many are the legal definitions of refugees provided by the United Nations High Commissioner for Refugees and many other organisations. However, none of these definitions would help us get more information on or better understand from a psychological perspective who the refugees are.

To properly analyse the issue of diversity and understand why this category is beneficial, we need to look at specific sub-categories of refugees: their location, age, background, gender, and family situation.

Speaking of refugees, especially in the media, we often talk about a faceless crowd in which an individual is very hardly seen. The idea of a faceless crowd usually connects to a specific perspective on the refugees: a victim perspective, an attitude of someone passive, who is just a victim, and that is the very opposite of the active, resilient, and agentic perspective. This is the first reason why differentiation is worth being recognised.

The second differentiation is that of refugees' specific location and background. As an example, the definition of "Syrian refugees" can easily describe rural Syrian families on the Syrian-Turkish border in Hatay or urban, single, and educated male refugees in Berlin or Istanbul.

The picture presented in figure 2[1] explains a lot about the category of refugees and the meaning of religion for them. This is a picture of twenty-five years old Iman, a Syrian mother forced from her home: when the photo was taken, she lived in a refugee camp in Turkey with her children. Her most precious possession was a copy of the Qur'an, which she said connected her to God.

Religion conveys not only a connection to God, but it can also connect refugees with their new locality.

Fig. 2: Iman, 25, with her son Ahmed and daughter Aishia, in Nizip refugee camp, Turkey. © Brian Sokol/UNHCR/Panos.

For example, a group of Syrian women who were urban refugees in Turkey told the interviewer that teaching their Turkish neighbours to read the Qur'an was a way of building a connection with the new locality (Grzymała-Moszczyńska 2019b). In this sense, religion supports resiliency as an adaptation to

---

1 See also: https://www.unhcr.org/spotlight/2019/05/most-important-thing-global/

a new situation and helps to regain agency in building bridges towards new neighbours.

However, a word of caution. We must be careful and remember that sometimes a local situation might contribute to a lack of support for refugees despite the shared religion between the refugees and locals. I am referring to my research in Aqaba (Jordan), where Syrian refugees living outside the camp were not supported, even in the way of offering some jobs to the boys or men by the local population. When asked why this happened, locals answered, "Well, you know… We have such hardships with finding jobs because of the economic situation in Jordan: we cannot afford to support refugees as well" (Grzymała-Moszczyńska 2019a).

Further on, another aspect that helps grasp the differences among refugees relates to the moment when the refugees are researched. Generally speaking, we can divide periods of refugeehood and the role of religion into three different time intervals: location, dislocation, and relocation. Location is when people are still in their place of origin. Dislocation is when people are running to safety. And relocation means people try to get new placement and get rooted in the new placement. Each of these contexts requires, supports or constricts resilience and agency of refugees and employs religion in a different capacity.

As field researchers, we very often encounter refugees just at a specific moment of their lives. We keep forgetting that they are connected to much more extended periods and more differentiated locations they went through before we met them, and that we have just a peek, a snapshot of their situation; we hardly ever follow the dynamic of the refugeehood process.

Speaking of location, the role of religion in the location where future refugees used to live is often boundary-making and stigmatising. Among people involved in ethnic cleansing, religion is the factor that causes them to be labelled as enemies; persecution and sometimes retaliation makes people fly from their local place. Also, religion can be used as an oppression tool to restore proper moral norms (e.g. in Chechnya, where military forces loyal to the pro-Russian government kidnap women and torture men because they call them infidels and justify their deeds by restoration of proper moral norms) (Grzymała-Moszczyńska 2018). Moreover, religion could be a tool for persecuting religious dissenters and atheists. The groups I have mentioned earlier, those of refugee artists and Scholars at Risk, are connected to this role of religion.

If people decide to flee the country, they enter the second period of refugeehood: dislocation. Different models help us understand the role of religion during dislocation (Miller and Rasmussen 2010).

The first one is the War Displacement Model. In this model, which is chiefly connected to disorders in migrants' functioning because of wartime trauma, violence, and loss, there is no referral to religion. Therefore, religion is not a factor which is taken into consideration.

In the second model, the Ecological Displacement-Related Model, religion appears in two roles, as the cage and as the bridge: it can help refugees join the new community, or it can act as a restrictive tool that keeps them on the side of enemies. Also, during the escape route, religion is often vital—and sometimes the only way— to help people retain hope in a hopeless situation. The Ecological Displacement Model considers not only dangerous flights but also dangerous refugee camps: once again, religion plays a double role as the bridge and the cage.

The third situation is relocation, described by the ADAPT (Adaptation and Development After Trauma and Persecution) Model created by Australian psychiatrist Derrick Silove (2013). Silove is the only scholar paying explicit attention to the role of religion as a possible tool, helping reconstruct the meaning of life through bridging past and present, old and new life. I think that is very important because religion gets its placement, which helps to understand why people need religion to get meaning in life after the traumas they experienced.

Figure 3 presents another picture which illustrates the value of the ADAPT Model[2]. This is a picture of a war refugee Elizabeth from Angola, living in the Democratic Republic of Congo, holding a Bible. She had been a refugee for fifty years, and the Bible was always with her. She explained that the Bible represented the connection to her previous life (she ran to safety from her hometown when she was only twenty) and also provided her with an explanation for all atrocities she experienced in life. She said: "In this world, bad things happen, but in the Bible, you can find words which will help you".

Elizabeth's story demonstrates how, in a situation of massive dislocation and relocation, religion can be a helpful tool in building a connection between the old and new life.

---

2   See also: https://www.unhcr.org/spotlight/2019/05/most-important-thing-global/.

Fig. 3: Elizabeth with her bible, Angola. © Brian Sokol/UNHCR/Panos.

We shall now look at how resilience, agency, and timing are interconnected.

Resilience is a precondition for restoring agency in refugees. Agency is a demonstration of resilience which—and that is interesting—is either wanted or refused at different stages of refugeehood. Agency is perceived as necessary at the moment of leave-taking and flight. It is desired when refugees arrive in the host country: they must be agentic to find a location and get the first safety measures. On the contrary, when the refugees are located in the reception centres or refugee camps, they are deprived of agency: refugees acquire an attitude of helplessness because an agentic refugee is a refugee who might be difficult to manage and might even expect some pressure and persecution from the camp personnel.

Finally, if agency is explicitly refused during the application procedure for humanitarian status, it must be again restored and become even wanted after receiving humanitarian protection.

If we look at agency from the perspective of refugees, intentionality, anticipation, self-reactivity, and self-reflection need to be recognised.

There are ongoing questions in the refugee interviews: "Who am I? Why am I here? What are my history, culture, and religion? In which way could I contribute to the community and other refugees? How can I remain myself? How can I oppose de-selfing (the erosion of agency due to external situations), and how can I oppose negative stereotypes because of my religion?" (Grzymała-Moszczyńska 2018).

The following example is about a sewing workshops conducted with Chechen women living in Poland[3]. In Chechen culture, how women dress is critical; therefore, helping them retain stylish attire despite poverty and limited funds is a way of helping them retain some agency. Sometimes refugees contribute to creating open local communities. Exquisite dresses, made for the female members of the choir of a Polish city, were jointly prepared by Chechen women relocated to that city and local ones. Chechen and Polish women were also sewing decorations for their houses on the Day of National Flag. Women were photographed even with the mayor of Gdansk, one of the cities where refugees retained agency the most by becoming recognised and legitimate partners of the City Council.

When the Covid19 pandemic started, Chechen refugees started crafting face masks and antiseptic gear for hospitals. It was when face masks were almost impossible to obtain in pharmacies or clinics. When I asked them, "Why? Why do you do so not just for yourself, but also for the community?" they answered, "We do not want to be forgotten; we still want to be present" (Grzymała-Moszczyńska 2020).

Back to deconstruction, one more step that has to be made in the service of diversity is the deconstruction of methodological paradigms and research methods from the perspective of resilience and agency.

When we talk about models of research among refugees, we can either refer to the so-called fly-in, fly-out approach or the approach based on the development of the relations. The fly-in, fly-out approach characterises quantitative methods. In this case, research methods aim to verify the hypothesis design to capture the Western understanding of religion, stress and copying using questionnaires and tests.

The second way of analysing religion and conducting research among refugees is based on developing relations. In this approach, research methods aim at understanding refugees' experiences and the role religion plays for them through interviews, focus group discussions, and drawings. Research, in this case, is much more oriented towards emic understanding or even indigenous cultural understanding from the point of view of a specific group of refugees.

Thanks to qualitative research, we are getting a better understanding of the role of religion in building resilience and agency; we can capture the simultaneous presence of multiple and contradictory experiences of refugees and, finally, make sense of the chaotic worlds that refugees are living in.

---

3 Foundation Women on the Road: https://www.kobietywedrowne.org/o-nas.

5 Conclusions

Religion contributes in both positive and negative ways to refugee trauma. Theoretical approaches tend to ignore such different kinds of impact because they are primarily grounded in quantitative research and do not accurately describe the context of cultures or religions outside the Western perspective.

The first important thing to remember would be not to assume who refugees are religion-wise because of their country of origin: we can recall the examples I already mentioned while speaking of Armenian Christians who come from a Muslim country, the Upper Karabakh enclave, or the Assyrian Christians coming from a Muslim country, like Syria.

A second important recommendation is always to check big data on refugee flows if you wish to understand their religiosity and look for additional sources of information.

And a final recommendation. Check the research methodology and methods behind findings about the relationship between the role of religion in coping with refugee trauma: respect diversity because it helps avoid simplistic assumptions, simplistic measures, and simplistic conclusions.

References

American Psychiatric Association. 1980. *Diagnostic and Statistical Manual of Mental Disorders*, Third Edition (DSM-III). Washington DC: American Psychiatric Association.

American Psychiatric Association. 2000. *Diagnostic and Statistical Manual of Mental Disorders*, Fourth Edition (DSM-IV-TR). Washington DC: American Psychiatric Association.

American Psychiatric Association. 2022. *Diagnostic and Statistical Manual of Mental Disorders*, Fifth Edition (DSM-V-TR). Washington DC: American Psychiatric Association.

Bandura, Albert. 1989. "Human Agency in Social Cognitive Theory." In *American Psychologist*, Vol. 44(9): 1175–1184.

Grzymała-Moszczyńska, Halina. 2018. Research Field Notes, Gdansk: Dom Międzykulturowy.

Grzymała-Moszczyńska, Halina. 2018. Research Field Notes.

Grzymała-Moszczyńska, Halina. 2019a. "Agency, Trauma, and Resilience: Yet Another Perspective on Refugee Experience." Cambridge: The Multilevel Governance of Migration, 17–19 October 2019 (conference paper).

Grzymała-Moszczyńska, Halina, and Maria Kanal. 2019b. "Research on Forced Migration from the Perspective of the Psychology of Religion: Opportunities and Challenges." In *Archive for the Psychology of Religion*, Vol. 41(3): 204–215.

Grzymała-Moszczyńska, Halina. 2020. Research Field Notes.

Lima, Luciano, Nassif, Vânia and Marcia Maria Garçon. 2020. "The Power of Psychological Capital: The Strength of Beliefs in Entrepreneurial Behavior,". In *RAC – Revista de Administração*

Contemporânea (Journal of Contemporary Administration), ANPAD – Associação Nacional de Pós-Graduação e Pesquisa em Administração, 24(4): 317–334.

Miller, Kenneth E. and Andrew Rasmussen. 2010. "War Exposure, Daily Stressors, and Mental Health in Conflict and Post-Conflict Settings: Bridging the Divide between Trauma-Focused and Psychosocial Frameworks". In *Social Science and Medicine*, Vol. 70(1): 7–16.

Silove, Derrick. 2013. "The ADAPT Model: A Conceptual Framework for Mental Health and Psychosocial Programming in Post Conflict Settings." In *Intervention*, Vol. 11(3): 237–248.

VandenBos, G. R. 2007. *APA Dictionary of Psychology*. American Psychological Association.

Halina Grzymała-Moszczyńska is Full Professor of Psychology at the Jesuit University Ignatianum in Cracow, Poland. She serves as Chair of the Department of Psychology of Religion and Spirituality and as President of the International Association for the Psychology of Religion since 2019. Her research and teaching areas are: psychology of migration (with 25 years of experience in refugee research); psychology of religion and spirituality. Grzymała-Moszczyńska most relevant recent publications are A. Anczyk, H. Grzymała-Moszczyńska (2021), *The Psychology of Migration: Facing Cultural and Religious Diversity*, Leiden-Boston: Brill; A. Anczyk, H. Grzymała-Moszczyńska, A. Krzysztof-Świderska, J. Prusak (2020), *Which Psychology(ies) Serves Us Best? Research Perspectives on the Psycho-Cultural Interface in the Psychology of Religion(s)*, Archive for the Psychology of Religion.

www.ingramcontent.com/pod-product-compliance
Lightning Source LLC
Chambersburg PA
CBHW052135010526
44113CB00036B/2270